A STONE FOR A PILLOW

Also by Madeleine L'Engle

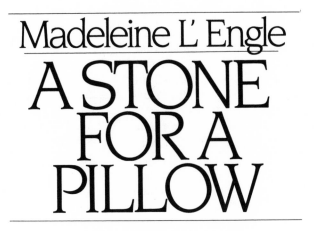

Madeleine L' Engle

A STONE FOR A PILLOW

Harold Shaw Publishers
Wheaton, Illinois

ISBN 0–87788–789–6

Cover photo: Gary Irving

Library of Congress Cataloging-in-Publication Data

L'Engle, Madeleine
    A stone for a pillow.

    1. Jacob (Biblical patriarch)   2. Christian life—
1960–   .   3. L'Engle, Madeleine.   I. Title.
BS580.J3E54   1986   222'.1106   86–6487
ISBN 0-87788-789-6

---

99   98   97   96   95   94
10   9   8   7   6

for
Marilyn, Gillian,
Margaret, and Libby

CONTENTS

Separation
from
the Stars

1

IN THE LATE AFTERNOON, when the long December night had already darkened the skies, we opened Christmas cards, taking turns, reading the messages, enjoying this once-a-year being in touch with far-flung friends. There, incongruously lying among the Christmas greetings, was an official-looking envelope addressed to me, with Clerk of Court, New York County, in the upper left hand corner. A call to jury duty. Manhattan does not give its prospective jurors much notice. My call was for the first week in January. To the notice inside had been added the words, *Must Serve.*

It wasn't the first time that my call had read *Must Serve.* A few months earlier I had written from Minnesota to the Clerk of Court, New York County, explaining that I was not trying to avoid jury duty, that I had previously served on a panel under a fine woman judge, and that I was ready and willing to serve again. But I pointed out, as I had already done several times before, that I do a good bit of lecturing which takes me far from New York, and I gave the Clerk of Court several dates when I would be available, sighing internally because bureaucracy never called me on the weeks that I offered.

This time they did.

So I relaxed and enjoyed Christmas in the country, at Crosswicks, bitter cold outside, warmth of firelight and candlelight within, and laughter and conversation and the delectable smells of roasting and baking. One of the highlights came on Christmas Day itself, with the mercury falling far below zero, when my husband went out into the winter garden and picked brussels sprouts, commenting as he brought them in triumphantly, "Mr. Birdseye never froze them like this," and we had brussels sprouts out of our own garden with Christmas dinner.

And then, before Twelfth-night, I was back in New York again, taking the subway downtown to the criminal court to which I had been assigned. I took plenty of work with me, because I had been told that lawyers do not like writers. But just as had happened on my previous jury duty, I got chosen as a juror on the second day. The case was an ugly one, involving assault in the second degree, which means possession of a dangerous weapon, with intent to cause injury or death.

Two men were sitting in the courtroom as defendants. They looked at the twelve of us who had been told to stay in our seats in the jury box—looked at us with cold eyes, with arrogance, even with contempt. Later, as we jurors got to know each other, we admitted that we were afraid of them. And yet, according to our judicial system, we had been put in the position of having to decide whether or not, according to the law, these men were guilty as charged.

I was fortunate to serve again under a highly intelligent woman judge, who warned us that we must set aside our emotions. What we felt about the defendants should not enter into our deliberations. We should not form any preconceived opinions. "And remember," she told us, "these two men and their lawyers do not have to prove to you that they are innocent. They do not have to appear on the witness stand. The burden of proof is on the assistant district attorney. The American way is that these two men are innocent, unless it can be proved, beyond a reasonable doubt, that they are guilty. This is the American way." She also pointed out that this assumption of innocence unless guilt can be proven is not the way of the rest of the world, of countries behind the Iron Curtain or in much of South America, where the assumption is that you are guilty unless, somehow or other, by persuasion or bribe, you can prove your innocence.

When I was called for jury duty, I knew that I would be taking two long subway rides each day, and riding the subway in Manhattan is nothing one does for pleasure. So I picked up a small book from one of my piles of Books To Be Read Immediately. Why did I pick this book at this particular time? I don't know. But I have found that often I will happen on a book just at the time when I most need to hear what it has to say.

This book couldn't have been more apt. It was *Revelation and Truth,* by Nicholas Berdyaev. I didn't do much reading the first day because I was sent from court to court, but once I was on a jury and had long periods of time in the jury room, I opened the book, surrounded by my fellow jurors who were reading, chatting, doing needlework or crossword puzzles. There couldn't have been a better place than a criminal court in which to read Berdyaev's words telling me that one of the gravest problems in the Western world today is that we have taken a forensic view of God.

Forensic: *to do with crime.* I first came across the word in an English murder mystery. Forensic medicine is medicine having to do with crime. The coroner needs to find out if the victim has been shot, stabbed, or poisoned. Was the crime accidental, self-inflicted, murder? Criminal medicine.

And there I was, in a criminal court, being warned by a

Russian theologian that God is not like a judge sentencing a criminal. Yet far too often we view God as an angry judge who assumes that we are guilty unless we can placate divine ire and establish our innocence. This concept seemed especially ironic after the judge's warning that this is not the American way of justice.

How did the Western world fall into such a gloomy and unscriptural misapprehension? Only a few weeks earlier I had participated in a teen-age TV show on the topic of religion. When the master of ceremonies asked the group of twenty or so bright high school students on the panel what they thought God looks like, I was horrified to hear them describe a furious old Zeus-figure with a lightning bolt in his hand. A forensic god.

Would this angry god, out to zotz us, have cared enough about us to come to us as Jesus of Nazareth, as a human, vulnerable baby? Or was it anger and not love at all that was behind the Incarnation, as a forensic view would imply? Did Jesus have to come and get crucified, because only if he died in agony could this bad-tempered father forgive his other children?

We got into a good discussion, then. The teen-agers did not really like their cartoon god. They were ready and willing to hear another point of view. We talked about astrophysics and particle physics and the interdependence of all of Creation. But I suspect there may have been in their minds a lingering shadow of God as a cold and unforgiving judge—not a judge who believes in the American way, but one who assumes our guilt.

But no, Berdyaev states emphatically, no, that is not God, not the God of Scripture who over and over again shows love for us imperfect creatures, who does not demand that we be good or virtuous before we can be loved. When we stray from God, it is not God's pleasure to punish us. It is God's pleasure to welcome us back, and then throw a party in celebration of our homecoming.

In Hosea God says,

All my compassion is aroused.
I will not carry out my fierce anger,
I will not destroy Ephraim again,
for I am God, not man:
I am the Holy One in your midst,
and have no wish to destroy.

The nature of God does not fluctuate. The One who made us is still the Creator, the Rejoicer, the Celebrator, who looks at what has been made, and calls it good.

✳ ✳ ✳

After the guard summoned us from the jury room to the court room, I sat in the jury box and looked at those two men who were there because they were destroyers rather than creators. They had used sharp knives, destructively; their intention had been to injure, or kill. I wasn't at all sure I wanted to be at the same celebration with them. They both had long hair, one head dark and greasy, the other brown and lank. They looked as though they had strayed out of the sixties, hippies who had grown chronologically, but not in any other way. It was difficult to abide by the judge's warning and not form any opinion of them until all the evidence was in.

That evening I was tired, mentally as well as physically. I bathed, then sat in my quiet corner to read Evening Prayer. For the Old Testament lesson I was reading the extraordinary story of Jacob's ladder of angels ascending and descending, linking earth and heaven, the Creation and the Creator, in glorious interdependence. The story of Jacob is not a story that can be interpreted forensically. It is not a tale of crime and corresponding punishment. Jacob is anything but a moral or virtuous character. He is a liar and a cheat. Heavenly visions do

13

not transform his conniving nature. The story of Jacob is unfair. He didn't get his just desserts. But do not turn to Scripture if you are looking for fairness!

When Jacob saw the ladder of angels he was fleeing Esau's legitimate outrage. He was afraid of his brother, and of God; that is, his father's and his grandfather's God. He had not yet made the decision to accept their God as his own.

But God stood above the ladder of angels, and said:

I am the Lord God of Abraham, your father, and the God of Isaac: the land that you are lying on, to you will I give it, and to your seed. And your seed shall be as the dust of the earth . . . And behold, I am with you, and will keep you in all the places where you go, and will bring you again to this land, for I will not leave you, until I have done that which I have said.

And Jacob woke out of his sleep, and he said, Surely the Lord is in this place, and I knew it not.

And he was afraid, and said, How dreadful is this place! This is none other than the house of God, and this is the gate of heaven.

For Jacob the house of God was not a building, not an enclosure, but an open place with earth for the floor, heaven for the roof. It would be several generations before the ark of God was built. For the early people of El Shaddai, the All Mighty One, any place where God spoke to them became the house of God.

So Jacob took the desert stone he had used for a pillow, and upon which he had dreamed the angelic dream, and set it up for a pillar, and poured oil upon the top of it. Oil—precious, sacramental. Today we can buy oils of all kinds, bath oil, olive oil, virgin oil, saturated and unsaturated oil. But to Jacob and his tribe, any oil was precious enough to make a significant sacrifice to El Shaddai and that sense of oil as sacramental and significant is retained today in my church as the healing oils are blessed each year.

Jacob called the place where he had set up the pillow-altar Beth-el—the house of God. Seekers and followers have sensed the Presence ever since, in circumstances that were often far from comfortable, as Luci Shaw suggests in her poem "Disciple" based on Luke 9:57–58:

Foxes lope home at dusk, each
to his sure burrow. Every bird
flies the twilight
to her down-lined nest.
Yet come with me to learn
a stern new comfort: the earth's
bed, me on guard at your side,
and, like pilgrim Jacob,
a stone for a pillow.

A stone for a pillow. It sounds odd to us, until we remember that very few people on this planet go to bed at night on soft pillows. In Japan the head-rest is often made of wood. In some countries it is simply the ground. I've tried a stone, not in bed, but late on a hot afternoon, when I call the dogs, and walk across the fields to the woods. Placed under the neck in just the right way, a stone can help me relax after a morning of typing—though I wouldn't want it for a whole night. But for a time to rest, to think, to let go and be, a warm, rounded stone can be a good pillow, reminding me that I am indeed in the house of God, that wherever I call upon my maker is always God's house.

When I was writing *And It Was Good*, reflections on the first chapters of Genesis, I found it helpful, when talking about the Creator, to use el (the first name by which the ancient

Hebrew called God), rather than the personal pronoun, she/he, him/her. I still find it helpful when thinking about the Maker of All Things. The personal pronoun was not a problem when it referred to the entirety of the human being, but we are presently living in a genitally-oriented culture, and I do not find it comfortable to limit God to the current sexual connotations and restrictions of the personal pronoun. Calling God *She* is just as sexist and limiting as calling God *He*.

It is fascinating that the conflict over God's sexuality comes at a time when pornography and sexual license are rampant. Even small cities have their massage parlors and "adult" book stores. This emphasis on the male and female genitals seems to be everywhere, even in our vision of the Creator.

Of course God is mother, nurturer, generator, as well as father, ruler, law-maker. But when we pound away with a sledge-hammer at God's sexuality (Ouch! but that is the image that comes to mind) we are seeing a God even more anthropomorphic than the God of the patriarchs.

In a universe which is becoming more and more varied as we discover more of the glories of the macrocosm and the infinite variety of the microcosm (are stars confined by gender? or quarks?), this preoccupation with God's sex seems amazingly primitive. But then, I suspect that we are still a pretty primitive people.

For all our mechanical and electronic sophistication, our thinking about ourselves and our maker is often unimaginative, egocentric, and childish. We need to do a great deal of growing up in order to reach out and adore a God who loves all of us with unqualified love.

But all those thousands of years ago when our forbears lived in the desert of an underpopulated and largely unexplored planet, the God of Jacob was definitely a masculine God, the Father God of the Patriarchs. So, when I am within Jacob's frame of reference, I'll return, for his story, to the masculine pronoun. But when I am lying on the rock in the late afternoon I am not in Jacob's time, or indeed not in any chronologic time at all, but in *kairos,* God's time, which touches on eternity.

I lie there quietly, lapped in peace, the blue of sky the ceiling, the stone under me the foundation, the trees forming arches rather than walls. The breeze is gentle, the sun not too hot; the stone is sun-warm and firm beneath me. Sometimes after dinner I go out to the rock known as the star-watching rock and wait for the stars to come out. There I can see all of Creation as the house of God, with the glory of the stars reminding me of the Creator's immensity, diversity, magnificence.

The stars are often referred to in Genesis. El Shaddai took Jacob's grandfather, Abraham, out into the desert night to show him the stars and to make incredible promises. How glorious those stars must have been all those centuries ago when the planet was not circled by a corona of light from all our cities, by smog from our internal combustion engines. Jacob, lying on the ground, the stone under his head, would have seen the stars as we cannot see them today. Perhaps we have thrown up a smoke screen between ourselves and the angels.

But Jacob would not have been blinded to the glory of the stars as part of the interdependence of the desert, the human being, the smallest insects, all part of Creation.

If we look at the makeup of the word disaster, dis-aster, we see *dis,* which means separation, and *aster,* which means star. So dis-aster is separation from the stars. Such separation is disaster indeed. When we are separated from the stars, the sea, each other, we are in danger of being separated from God.

Sometimes the very walls of our churches separate us from God and each other. In our various naves and sanctuaries we are safely separated from those outside, from other denominations, other religions, separated from the poor, the ugly, the dying. I'm not advocating pulling down the walls of our churches, though during the activist sixties I used to think it might be a good idea if we got rid of all churches which seat more than two hundred. But then I think of the huge cathedral which is my second home in New York, and how its great stone arms welcome a multitude of different people, from the important and affluent to waifs and strays and the little lost ones of a great, overcrowded city. We need to remember that the house of God is not limited to a building that we usually visit for only a few hours on Sunday. The house of God is not a safe place. It is a cross where time and eternity meet, and where we are—or should be—challenged to live more vulnerably, more interdependently. Where, even with the light streaming in rainbow colours through the windows, we can listen to the stars.

Stars have always been an icon of creation for me. During my high school years, when I was at my grandmother's beach cottage for vacations, I loved to lie on a sand dune and watch the stars come out over the ocean, often focussing on the brilliant grace of one particular star. Back in school, I wrote these lines:

I gaze upon the steady star
That comes from where I cannot see,
And something from that distant far

Pierces the waiting core of me
And fills me with an aweful pain
That I must count not loss but gain.

If something from infinity
Can touch and strike my very soul,
Does that which comes from out of me
Reach and pierce its far off goal?

Very young verses, but they contain the germ of an understanding of the interdependence of all Creation.

After I was out of college, living in New York and working

on my first novel, I was so hungry for stars that I would take the subway up to the Planetarium and connect myself to the stars that way. My distress at being separated from the stars is not something esoteric or occult; it is a symptom of separation from Creation and so, ultimately, from community, family, each other, Creator.

✳ ✳ ✳

That January evening after the first tiring day as a juror, after I had read the story of Jacob and the angels, I turned to the New Testament, to read from the ninth chapter of Matthew's Gospel, where Jesus had called Matthew from collecting taxes. In Israel in those days, a tax collector worked for the hated Romans, rather than for an equivalent of the I.R.S. We don't have any analogy for the kind of tax collector Matthew was. But because they were employed by the enemy, all tax collectors were scum.

Nevertheless, incredibly, Jesus called Matthew to be one of his disciples, and that night he went for dinner to his house, where there were more tax collectors, and various other kinds of social outcasts, and the censorious Pharisees asked the disciples, "Why does your master eat with tax collectors?"

Jesus heard the question and said, "It is not the healthy who need a doctor, but the sick. Go and learn the meaning of the words, *What I want is mercy, not sacrifice.*" He was quoting from the prophet, Hosea. And he went on, "And indeed I have not come to call the virtuous, but sinners."

I'm uneasy about self-conscious virtue. It implies that the virtuous person is in control, keeps all the laws, has all the answers, always knows what is right and what is wrong. It implies a conviction which enables the virtuous person to feel saved, while the rest of the world is convicted.

Probably it was because I was on jury duty that I noticed the paradoxical connections between the words conviction, convince, convicted, *con*vict (noun), and con*vict* (verb). If we assume that we are virtuous, particularly when we set our virtue against someone else's sin, we are proclaiming a forensic, crime-and-punishment theology, not a theology of love. The Pharisees who did not like to see Jesus eating with sinners wanted virtue—virtue which consisted in absolute obedience to the law.

The Pharisees were not bad people, remember. They were good. They were virtuous. They did everything the Moral Majority considers moral. They knew right from wrong, and they did what was right. They went regularly to the services in the temple. They tithed, and they didn't take some off the top for income tax or community services or increased cost-of-living expenses. They were, in fact, what many Christians are calling the rest of us to be: good, moral, virtuous, and sure of being saved.

So what was wrong? Dis-aster. Separation from the stars, from the tax collectors, the Samaritans, from the publican who beat his breast and knew himself to be a sinner. The Pharisees, not all of them, but some of them, looked down on anybody who was less moral, less virtuous than they were. They assumed that their virtue ought to be rewarded and the sin of others punished.

If we twelve jurors found those two men guilty as charged, they would be punished by the state. They would likely be put in prison: forensic punishment. Necessary in our judicial system, perhaps, but Berdyaev warned that we should not think of God's ways as being judicial. God is a God of love.

When I looked at those two cruel-faced men I had to remind myself that they were God's children, and that they were loved. If they had committed the crime of which they were accused, it would cause God grief, not anger.

The three patriarchs must have caused El Shaddai considerable grief. If Jacob was a cheat, it ran in the family. Abraham, Isaac, and Jacob had much in common—long lives, many wives, children born late to the barren but beloved wife, and a shrewdness which did not shrink from cheating.

Jacob's grandfather, Abraham, who had been called by God from the comforts of home into the dangers of a strange land, pretended to King Abimelech of Gerar that his wife, Sarah, was his sister. According to the custom of that place and time, Abimelech or one of his men could "know" the stranger's sister. But if they wanted his wife, then, according to custom, they would have to kill the husband.

Abimelech uncovered Abraham's deception, and then, a generation later, we have almost the same story, with Isaac, Abraham's son, pretending that Rebekah is his sister, not his wife, in order to protect his own skin. And again Abimelech discovers the deception.

"Why did you do this to me?" he demands.

"So you wouldn't kill me," Isaac answers. Isaac, like Abraham, his father, was willing to sacrifice his beautiful wife's honour to these powerful men in order to save his own life. Evidently both Sarah and Rebekah went along with the deception, but whether willingly or unwillingly we are not told. Many things were different in those days, particularly the position of women.

✳ ✳ ✳

In order for us to know Jacob and to think about his story, it is helpful to remember his family tree. Jacob was the third of the three patriarchs. The first was Abraham.

Abraham and his wife, Sarah, had a son, Isaac.

Isaac and his wife, Rebekah, had twin sons, Esau and Jacob.

Isaac never seemed to question the fact that his father Abraham's God was also his God. But Jacob was a more complicated character than his father. It took him considerable time and several incredible encounters with the divine Presence before he decided to accept as his own God the God of his father, Isaac, and his grandfather, Abraham. He tried to bargain with God, but he found that his bargaining did not work. Ultimately he dropped all his deviousness and cheating and, naked before God, accepted El Shaddai.

Isaac, a far more direct person than his son, was acted *on* more often than he was allowed to act. Abraham actually raised the knife to offer Isaac as a sacrifice. He also chose Isaac's wife for him, and although Isaac came to love Rebekah, he had no say in the choosing of her. And yet Isaac knew himself to be singled out by God, and he remained faithful to this God who made promises as splendid as the star-filled sky.

The God of the Patriarchs belonged to a people, rather than to a place. El Shaddai, their God, was one god among many gods, the varied and various deities of the surrounding tribes. Throughout the Old Testament, there are numerous references to other gods, and to "our" God as the greatest of these. Whose God is like our God? There is no other God like our God. "Who is he among the gods, that shall be like unto the Lord?" asks the psalmist.

The chief difference between the God of Abraham, Isaac, and Jacob, and the gods of the other tribes, was that El Shaddai cared for, loved his people, and did not stand apart from them and demand constant blood sacrifices. It was the other gods who were forensic. Jacob's God was the God who was *in* the story. It is only slowly, as we move through Scripture, that this God among many gods becomes the God who is One, the God who is All. The human being's attempt to understand the Creator is never static; it is constantly in motion. If we let our concept of God become static, and we have done so over and over again throughout history, we inevitably blunder into a forensic interpretation, and that does not work.

In a vain attempt to make people see God as an avenging judge, theologians have even altered the meaning of words. Atonement, for instance. A bad word, if taken forensically.

A young friend said to me during Holy Week, "I cannot cope with the atonement."

Neither can I, if the atonement is thought of forensically. In forensic terms, the atonement means that Jesus had to die for us in order to atone for all our awful sins, so that God could forgive us. In forensic terms, it means that God cannot forgive us unless Jesus is crucified and by this sacrifice atones for all our wrongdoing.

But that is not what the word means! I went to an etymological dictionary and looked it up. It means exactly what it says, at-one-ment. I double-checked it in a second dictionary. There is nothing about crime and punishment in the makeup of that word. It simply means to be at one with God. Jesus on the cross was so at-one with God that death died there on Golgotha, and was followed by the glorious celebration of the Resurrection.

Our legal system has to be forensic. We have laws, Paul points out, because we have sin. And what is sin? It is not frivolous to say that sin is discourtesy.

✳ ✳ ✳

Discourtesy. I sat in the jury room with the radiators hissing and the January cold pressing against the windows, hearing the constant sound of taxis and busses and cars honking on the streets below, and thought of Crosswicks, our house outside a village so small that it doesn't have traffic lights. In New York, without lights, our traffic would be in an even worse mess than it is. I was amazed when I was at St. Scholastica College in Duluth, Minnesota, to find a city so small that there were few traffic lights, and at the intersections cars courteously took turns. By and large, drivers across the United States are not that courteous. So we need traffic lights.

Sin, then, is discourtesy pushed to an extreme, and discourtesy is lack of at-one-ment. If you drive your car without any thought for the other drivers on the road, you are separating yourself. To be discourteous is to think only of yourself, and not of anybody else. The result of this "me, myself, and I"-ism leads to the horror of drivers who will hit animals—or human beings—and callously drive on. Dis-aster. Separation. Atonement reversed and shattered. And so crime increases in the anonymity of our cities, as does drunkenness and drug-taking and stealing and raping and killing, and as a result we have our judicial system, and the criminal courts. In that dusty little jury room I understood Paul's comment that we have laws because we have sin. Dis-aster. But the stories of Abraham, Isaac, and Jacob precede the coming of the Law, and there was for the patriarchs, despite their cheating and lying, an innocence in their encounters with God that got lost with laws, with crime and punishment.

If we on the panel found those two men guilty, the state would punish them, but I'm not at all sure that this forensic type of punishment is punishment at all. It may be deterrence, or an attempt to protect the innocent. I have no desire to go all wishy-washy and bleeding-heart about the rapist who is let off with an easy sentence so that he can then go out and rape and kill again, as statistics prove is almost inevitable. Our jails may be deplorable, our courts overcrowded and years behind schedule; our lawyers are not knights in shining armour; but we do what we can, in our blundering way, to curb crime and violence, and our top-heavy system remains one of the best on the planet.

But our own need for law and our system of prosecution and sentencing does not produce true punishment, because true punishment should result in penitence. Real punishment produces an acceptance of wrongdoing, a repugnance for what has been done, confession, and an honest desire to amend. Real punishment comes to me when I weep tears of grief because I have let someone down. The punishment is not inflicted by anyone else. My own recognition and remorse for what I have done is the worst punishment I could possibly have.

Jacob punished himself after tricking Esau. His terror of

revenge made him run away from his brother, and it was to be many years before he could return home.

Perhaps the most poignant moment for me in all of Scripture comes after Peter has denied Jesus three times, and Jesus turns and looks at him. That loving look must have been far worse punishment for Peter than any number of floggings. And he went out and wept bitterly.

Jacob, too, learned to weep bitterly, but he was an old man before he came to an understanding of himself which included acceptance of repentance without fear.

This is something a criminal court is not equipped to cope with. The judge and the lawyers and the jurors are there to learn the facts as accurately as possible, and to interpret them according to the law. Forensically.

It is impossible to interpret the story of Jacob in this way. Jacob does outrageous things, and instead of being punished, he is rewarded. He bargains with God shamelessly:

"*If* God will be with me, and will keep me in this way that I go, and will give me bread to eat, and raiment to put on, so that I come again to my father's house in peace; *then* shall the Lord be my God."

Jacob also agrees to tithe, but only if God does for him all that he asks. He cheats, but he knows that he cheats; he never tries to fool himself into thinking that he is more honest than he is. He openly acknowledges his fear of Esau's revenge.

And yet, with all his shortcomings, he is a lovable character, and perhaps we recognize ourselves in him with all his complexity. He has an extraordinary sense of awe—an awe which does not demand fairness, an awe which is so profound a response to the Creator that it cannot be sustained for long periods of time.

But whenever El Shaddai came to Jacob, he was ready for the Presence. That was why he took his stone pillow and built an altar. Jacob knew delight in the Lord in a spontaneous manner which too many of us lose as we move out of childhood. And because we have forgotten delight, we are unable to accept the golden light of the angels.

Three centuries ago Thomas Traherne wrote:

> Should God give Himself and all worlds to you, and you refuse them, it would be to no purpose. Should he love you and magnify you, should he give his son to die for you, and command all angels and men to love you, should He exalt you in His throne and give you dominion over all his works and you neglect them, it would be to no purpose.
>
> Should he make you in His image, and employ all his Wisdom and power to fill eternity with treasures, and you despise them, it would be in vain. In all these things you have to *do;* and therefore all your actions are great and magnificent, being of infinite importance in all eyes; while all creatures stand in expectation of what will be the result of your liberty . . . It is by your love that you enjoy all his delights, and are delightful to him.

As I live with Jacob's story I see that there is far more to him than the smart cheat, the shallow manipulator. There are many times when he so enjoyed the delights of God, that he himself became delightful.

How often are we delightful to God? How marvellous that we are called to be delightful!

We are not meant to cringe before God, or to call on Jesus to come and save us from an angry and vengeful Father. We are to enjoy all the delights which the Lord has given us, sunsets and sunrises, and a baby's first laugh, and friendship and love, and the brilliance of the stars. Enjoying the Creator's delights implies connectedness, not dis-aster.

And so there is hope that we, too, may so enjoy all the delights that God has given us, that we may truly be delightful.

The Butterfly Effect

2

ALMOST EVERY EARLY SPRING we have ice storms around Crosswicks. While the mercury hovers around the freezing point, the rain falls and as it touches the trees it coats the branches with silver, bending the birches like bows, drooping the delicate twigs of willow and maple with a heavy freight of ice. Inside the old walls of Crosswicks the wood stoves and the open fireplace keep us warm, and when the ice-laden power lines fall, candles and oil-lamps are lit.

The power usually goes out during an ice storm, so since our pump is powered by electricity, at the first sign of freezing rain we fill the tubs, and several kettles of water. During our first ice storm we were not country-wise enough to prepare for waterlessness, and caught cold by having to go outdoors in the icy rain to relieve ourselves. Since then, while the power is out, we flush the toilet once or twice a day by filling a bucket with water from the tub, and sloshing it down the bowl. This used to fascinate the children, who wanted us to flush the toilet more often than we thought necessary. After all, that tub of water had to last us until the power came back on.

One time, many years ago when the children were little, an ice storm came at the time of the full moon. We went to bed with nothing to see in the sky but thick clouds, and we listened to the progressive sounds of rain, the clicking of ice, and the sudden loud cracking of broken branches. During the night the wind shifted from the east to the northwest. The clouds had been ripped away and the full moon was revealed, bringing the ice-coated branches to life with silver and diamonds. It was a faerie land of beauty, and we woke the children, so that they would not miss the extraordinary loveliness.

Ice storms are magically beautiful, but they also cause great damage to the trees, which cannot withstand the weight of ice. Such storms are part of the normal expectations of wind and rain as the earth begins to thaw from the long winter freeze.

But the weather also does things which are not at all anticipated. On the last Monday of June a twister pranced by our house, which was neither expected nor usual. Throughout most of the area there was no more than an ordinary summer thunder storm, not particularly severe. But along one lethal path there was a tornado. Fortunately we were all out, and all the windows were wide open to catch the breeze. Otherwise, I am told, we might not still *have* a house.

On the little terrace outside our kitchen windows are some fairly heavy chairs, deliberately heavy, because a house on a hill is vulnerable to high winds. One of the chairs was tossed across the road, along with a couple of small tables. Branches of the old willow tree were found twisted in the limbs of a maple tree on the other side of the garden. In the orchard our favourite old winesap apple tree was snapped off at the roots and lay dying on the ground. A majestic maple was felled and crashed across the road. Another maple was split from top to bottom, sliced in half. Almost all the trees lost major branches. The ground was littered with limbs and leaves and with hail the size of golf balls. It was a scene of devastation.

And we ourselves were devastated. It was an abrupt reminder of the precariousness of this world full of the Creator's delights. After the separation of the creature from the created when Adam and Eve were sundered from the Garden, the world has been unstable under our feet. There seems to be no spot on earth which is immune to the "natural disasters" of tornado, hurricane, earthquake. In northwest Connecticut we must often batten down against hurricanes, but a tornado in our part of the world seemed an unnatural disaster, leaving us bewildered.

The only reason we had a vegetable garden left was the unusually cold spring which delayed planting, and the tender shoots of corn and tomato, broccoli and green pepper, were still tiny. They were lashed to the ground by wind and rain, but they were young enough so that they could be lifted upright again, take deeper root, and grow.

All during the summer we stiffened nervously whenever we heard a rumble of thunder, and looked at the horizon to make sure there was no dark funnel of cloud rolling towards us. But the precariousness of the planet next manifested itself not in a storm but in the trembling of the earth. I woke up one early autumn morning just after dawn, feeling the bed shaking under me. Earthquakes are not common in the Litchfield Hills, but there was no doubt that this was an earthquake, rattling the windows, shaking the floors.

It was not a severe earthquake, though it was an unusually long one, and it again left us with a renewed awareness of the uncertainty of life. We never know, from one moment to the next, what is going to happen.

The psalmist sings, "God is our refuge and strength, a very present help in trouble. Therefore we will not fear, though the earth be moved, and though the hills be carried into the midst of the sea; though the waters rage and swell, and though the mountains shake in the tempest."

On one level that is true. To know that we are one with our Maker gives us this deep understanding that el is indeed our hope and our strength. But there is another level in us that legitimately experiences fear when the earth is moved, or the hills fall, or the tempest rages.

Earthquakes were more common when the planet was younger, and the earth's crusts were still settling. In Jacob's desert world there was a newness and a harshness to the land, shrivelling under the fiery sun. Famine was more lethal than storm, and Jacob came to know famine in much the same way that it is being known in desert countries today, where the rains are not falling, and the sands move across and choke a once green and fertile land.

My mother, who was a very wise woman, used to say that when we abuse the planet overmuch, it will turn on us. Is that what is happening, with earthquakes, floods, droughts, volcanic erruptions devastating the earth? We have not wondered enough at the delights God has given us to appreciate them, and be good stewards. We have overworked the land, poured pollutants into river and stream, fouled the air we breathe with gas fumes and chemical smoke spiralling up from industrial chimneys. We have sown the wind. We are reaping the whirlwind.

Cleaning up after the tornado was a sad job. A fleeting thought crossed my mind: We have faithfully tended our little corner of field and forest, we plough compost back into the garden in the autumn, we use no chemical fertilizers or sprays, we try to keep the woods a safe haven for wild life. We plant and nurture trees and flowers and vegetables and herbs. But if we expect that to protect us from wind and storm, aren't we falling into forensic thinking again? Aren't we crying out, in effect, "But it's not fair!"

We cut and piled wood from the wind-felled trees, knowing that they would provide more than enough firewood for the winter, but still grieving for the death of those trees which had been our friends.

I like to take time out to listen to the trees, much in the same way that I listen to a sea shell, holding my ear against the rough bark of the trunk, hearing the inner singing of the sap. It's a lovely sound, the beating of the heart of a tree.

I couldn't stop myself from asking, Why the old apple tree? Why the grand maples? Why did the twister skip the ancient willow, fading with age, or a sapling which wasn't doing well, and attack the strongest and healthiest trees? If the tornado was not consciously evil, it was still evil.

I wrestle with these questions which do not have logical answers, wrestle with mysteries, much as Jacob wrestled with the angel. How do we even attempt to understand the meaning of tempest and tragedy, love and hate, violence and peace?

I struggle, and as always when I struggle to find the truth of something, I turn to story for illumination. And, as I grapple with the angels of difficult questions, I think of Jacob who saw a ladder of angels, reaching from earth to heaven, with the angels of God ascending and descending, linking heaven and earth, the creation to the Creator, not separated from each other, but participating in each other. Delight. At-one-ment.

For God is beyond all our forensic thinking. God is Love.

During the first week of jury duty I got home one night as the phone was ringing. With no sense of foreboding I picked it up, and a cold and angry voice accused me of spreading abroad a terrible secret I had been told in deepest confidence. I had told no one. I do not know how the secret—so terrible I cannot even hint at it—leaked out, who else had been told. But I was blamed, and I was angry, very angry, at the injustice of the accusation. How could the person who had trusted me enough to tell such a devastating story then turn around and think that

I was the kind of person who would abuse and betray such trust?

In my outrage, I wanted justice to be done. I wanted to be exonerated. I wanted whomever it was who had viciously spread the secret to be caught and punished. Forensic thinking—and I needed to grapple with this, not angrily, but lovingly, compassionately. Jury duty and Jacob had pushed me into some hard thinking.

Jacob's brother, Esau, also went through outrage at the injustice which had been done him, but he did not remain in anger. He wept in anguish over the lack of justice, but he did not sulk.

Family stories are as complicated in the great dramas of Scripture as they are in real life. A few weeks ago, after a large family gathering, I wrote in my journal with a figurative sigh of relief that nothing untoward had happened, adding that with a family as complex as ours, that was no small achievement. But honest family relations are seldom simple. Isaac must often have grieved about his twin sons. And what kind of image did Isaac himself have of fathers? What did he think of his own father who had bound him and laid him on the wood for the holocaust, and lifted his knife to kill him? What did Isaac think of a father/God who would ask such a thing even if, at the last moment, this masculine God sent a ram in a bush for a reprieve? If Jacob was slow to accept Isaac's God for his own, it would surely be understandable for Isaac to be slow to accept Abraham's God, but there is no indication that he was reluctant. He was an extraordinarily accepting man.

I must learn to accept, too. To accept that life is not fair. That I must not remain in my hurt and anger over being falsely accused of betrayal. That I must let it go, and move on, as best I can. As the people of Scripture were willing to let go and move on, to go wherever it was that God called them.

Poor Isaac, Jacob's father. His life was not easy. Probably the best part of it was his love for Rebekah, even if Abraham chose her for him. But the meeting of Isaac and Rebekah is the first love story in the Bible—love story, rather than romance, for "romantic love" was non-existent in the harsh and practical realities of desert life when the nomadic Hebrews were wandering from oasis to oasis. That is just as well, for romantic love is not real love. The illusion of romantic love as something pure and undying kills the possibility of real love. Romantic love inevitably leads to death. Tristan and Isolde, Pelleas and Melisande, Héloise and Abelard: theirs was romantic love, magnificent romantic love, perhaps, but it led to death. There is also a creative death to romantic love, the death to the illusory love of romance, and a growing up to the true love of mature human beings.

The great teacher at Smith, Mary Ellen Chase, told our class that the novel begins where the romance and the fairy tale end.

The patriarchs and matriarchs, Abraham and Sarah, Isaac and Rebekah, Jacob and Rachel, had the real thing, despite their human foibles, and their human sins. Having seen the great Sahara desert, I understand something of the incredible physical demands made of husband and wife in that unfriendly climate. They had to be able to work together, to be good companions. A love which was romantic or merely erotic would never have survived.

Isaac had need of a good companion, especially after Sarah, his mother, died. In those days the genuine love of mother and son was not considered neurotic, nor need it be at any time. It was Isaac's father, not his mother, who bound him and laid him on the altar of the rock. It was the incomprehensible Father/God who gave the order for the holocaust. Perhaps Sarah would have refused?

Even after the substitution of the ram, Isaac may have had twinges of wonder about the reliability of fathers. Maybe fathers were expected to be unreliable. But Sarah, the mother, was to be counted on, in laughter, in tears, to accept even where she did not condone. Isaac must have missed her grievously.

And in those days people had not yet fallen into the "blame it all on your parents" syndrome, a misconception as fallacious as the illusion of romantic love. It insists that nothing is our fault, thereby denying us any share in the writing of our own story. Whatever we have done that is wrong is considered to be not our fault because of our parents. Or our teachers. Or somebody. When we refuse all responsibility for our behaviour by blaming it on our parents (or anybody else), we are also abdicating free will. A lot of us (I, too), have had unhappy or strange childhoods, but this need not be lethally crippling. Isaac rose above all that had happened to him and became one of the trinity of patriarchs invoked as Israel's heroes.

And as helpmeet he had Rebekah.

The story of Abraham's search for a wife for Isaac emphasizes that there will be trouble if one marries someone who worships an alien god. Therefore Abraham did not want Isaac to marry someone from the land of Canaan, in which they had settled, and where the gods were not El Shaddai. So Abraham called to himself the eldest servant of his household and said to him, "I am asking you to put your hand under my thigh." (By this Abraham's servant and friend knew that he was being asked to make the most solemn oath possible, because special veneration was given the organs of generation.)

Abraham continued,

> I ask you to swear by the Lord, the God of heaven, and the God of earth, that you will not let my son marry a daughter of the Canaanites, among whom we live. No. You are to go back to my country, and to my kind, and find a wife among them for my son, Isaac.
>
> The servant said, "But perhaps the woman will not be willing to come with me to this strange land. Then would

you want me to bring your son back to the land you came from?"

Abraham said, "No! Do not take my son back there. The Lord God of heaven, who took me from my father's house, and from the land of my own people, and who spoke to me, and who swore to me, saying, 'To your seed will I give this land,' this Lord my God will send an angel before you, and you will be able to bring back a wife for my son."

Arranged marriages continue in a good many parts of the world to this day; it is only in our century in the Western world that they have become a thing of the past. How could a marriage arranged by God and his angel fail? Isaac and Rebekah loved each other from the start.

Love stories in the Bible tend to begin at a well, the common meeting place for nomads. Abraham's servant went to the well in Aram-Naharaim—all the way back to Mesopotamia in the northwest. A young woman appeared, and drew water for the servant and for his camels. The servant asked her name, and when he learned that she was Rebekah, a young woman of Abraham's tribe, he gave her the jewels Abraham had sent with him, and she hurried home with the news of the stranger's arrival.

Laban, Rebekah's brother, came out to meet Abraham's servant, to give him food, and to make marriage negotiations. Laban, the negotiator. Years later, when Jacob fled to him and fell in love with his daughter, Rachel, he was a party to many more elaborate negotiations.

Laban agreed to the marriage of his sister, Rebekah, with Isaac. Rebekah, too, agreed, although she had never set eyes on the young man, and she set out with Abraham's servant to go to the land of Canaan.

Isaac appeared to have had no objection to having a marriage arranged for him. One evening, while Abraham's servant had not yet returned from his mission, Isaac went out into the fields to meditate. To meditate on the strange events of his life. On the wonder of the desert stars, and the incomprehensible maker of them all. Dis-aster was not for him. He was connected to the stars, and to the land, and to the tribe. While he was alone, meditating, he lifted up his eyes, and saw camels coming toward him. And he saw Rebekah.

Rebekah, in her turn, saw Isaac, and asked who the young man was. Abraham's servant told her that it was Isaac, to whom she was betrothed.

Her heart must have lifted, for it was a brave thing for Rebekah to do, to leave her family and go to a strange land to be the bride of a young man she had never seen. Even though such was the custom of her people, it was still courageous. But as the story continues, it is apparent that Rebekah did not lack courage.

So Isaac took Rebekah for his wife, "and he loved her, and Isaac was comforted after his mother's death." Abraham, too, comforted himself; he married again, despite his advanced age, and had several more children. But, according to the story, it was to Isaac that Abraham gave everything he had.

And then Abraham died.

Isaac, and his half brother, Ishmael, buried their father. Isaac, the legitimate son of Abraham and Sarah, was the favourite. Ishmael was the child of Hagar, Sarah's handmaid, according to the custom of the time. Hagar's scorn of barren Sarah began a bitterness which only death could heal, and it is comforting to think that these two alienated brothers were reconciled, and that together they buried their father. They had played together as children. They came together as men, with their father's death binding them, salving the old hurts. The schism caused by Hagar's arrogance and Sarah's resentment was finally healed.

There was no denial of death in those days of a sparsely-populated land. Now we hide it away in nursing homes and hospitals, prolong it, often painfully, with life-support systems. But for Isaac and Ishmael, birth and death were a natural part of life, and unless someone was killed by a wild animal or in an unforeseen accident, death was prepared for openly. I hope that the two brothers, together at last, were able to hold each other's hands as well as their father's. Now, in the bloody world of the Middle East, it is time for Isaac and Ishmael to clasp hands again. In the world of Islam, Ishmael is revered above Isaac but they laughed together as children, and God heard them both and loved them.

* ✳ *

At Crosswicks we are dependent on a well for our water. But it was not until I stood on the sands of the Sahara that I consciously understood the importance of wells for the people of the desert, where the sun scorches the parched land and the sand blows constantly.

Before our trip to Egypt I read that people who wear contact lenses should leave them at home, the blowing sand is so pervasive. Since I do not see without contact lenses, leaving them at home was not an option for me, so I bought a pair of swimming goggles to wear over my contacts! On the day that we went to see the Sphinx and the great pyramids the wind rose, and we were caught in a sand storm. I was more than grateful for my swimming goggles; they protected my eyes from the stinging sand far more effectively than ordinary spectacles would have, and while everybody else ran for cover, I was able to watch the strange beauty of the storm until the force of the sand, blowing in horizontal waves, stung my legs like shot and finally drove me to shelter.

No wonder women wear veils in that part of the world. The veils protect them not only from men's eyes, but from the blowing sand.

A well provides not only water for drink, but irrigation for keeping an oasis green. A well is necessary for life.

When Abimelech sent Isaac away from Gerar, saying, "Go from us, for you are mightier than we are," Isaac's first priority was finding water. He pitched his tent in the valley of Gerar, and his servants dug in the valley, and found there a well of springing water. And the herdsmen of Gerar fought with Isaac's herdsmen, saying, "The water is ours." So Isaac's herdsmen dug another well, and there was a battle over that one, too. So they went further and dug yet another well, and no one tried to take that one away from them, and Isaac called the name of it Rehoboth, and he said, "For now the Lord has made room for us, and we shall be fruitful in the land." And the Lord appeared to him that night and said, "I am the God of Abraham, your father; fear not, for I am with you, and will bless you, and multiply your seed for my servant Abraham's sake."

'And Isaac built an altar there, and called upon the name of the Lord, and pitched his tent, and there his servants dug yet another well.'

Digging a well in the desert is no easy chore. Water is not always reached at the first dig, or the second, or even the third. And often the digging has to be very deep before a spring is reached. But they succeeded in digging a well.

Then Abimelech came from Gerar, with two of his chief warriors, and Isaac said, "Why have you come to me, after you have sent me away from you?"

And Abimelech and his warriors said, "We saw certainly that the Lord is with you. Let there now be an oath between us, and let us make a covenant together, that you will do us no hurt. We have not hurt you, we have done only good to you, and we sent you away in peace. And we see now that you are the blessed of the Lord."

And Isaac made them a feast, and they ate and drank together, and in the morning they rose early and swore to

each other, and Isaac sent them away, and they departed
from him in peace.

Isaac wanted peace. When he married Rebekah he must have
thought that at last his life was going to move in quiet ways of
love, harmony, and prosperity. Their marriage was one of deep
love, but Rebekah had no children. Since it was the woman
who carried and bore the children, it was assumed that the
woman was at fault if the marriage was not blessed by babies.
Childlessness was a source of humiliation to a woman. Rebekah's
childlessness must have seemed a bitter irony to Isaac, who had
been born so late in his parents' lives that they could have been
his grandparents. How amazing was this God who had brought
Abraham and Sarah to this strange country, who had given Sarah
a baby in her old age, and then almost taken him away in that
extraordinary demand for blood sacrifice! Now what was this
God going to do about that rash promise that Abraham's descendants, through Isaac, would be as numerous as the stars in the
sky? What kind of a jokester God was this?

Perhaps Isaac had mixed feelings about the Creator of the
universe, of the countless stars in the heavens, of the grains of
sand in the desert, and of strange promises. But he entreated
God, as the Hebrew patriarchs never hesitated to do, and at
last he and Rebekah were given twin sons.

Rebekah had a difficult pregnancy:

The children struggled with one another inside her, and she
said, "If this is the way of it, why go on living?"
  So she went to consult the Lord, and he said to her,
    There are two nations in your womb.
    Your issue will be two rival peoples,
    One nation shall have the mastery of the other,
    and the elder shall serve the younger.

The descendants of Esau were to be the Edomites, and those of Jacob the Israelites, and there was indeed to be enmity between them.

I wonder if Rebekah was sorry she had consulted the Lord? This was a hard prediction to carry with her through the rest of her pregnancy.

When the time came for her confinement, there were indeed twins in her womb, and a rough birthgiving, two babies, one coming immediately after the other, the younger grabbing his twin's heel. Esau, the first born, was covered with red hair like a little animal. Jacob, the heel-grabber, was a fraternal twin, smooth-skinned and far from identical.

As they grew, Esau became a hunter, and Isaac's favourite son. Jacob tended the land around the home tent, and was loved by Rebekah.

In *The Parable of the Tribes,* Alexander Schmookler points out that the world of the hunter was moderately peaceable. It was a sparsely populated world. If the human being was to survive, interdependence was essential. It was only when one tribe grew stronger than other neighbouring tribes, had more children, cattle, goats, and camels, that trouble began, as was the case with Isaac and Abimelech. "The rise of agriculture made possible a more settled life with far larger populations living in the same territory."

When wells were dug, and water made more available, the tribe tended to settle around the well. So, when Isaac's wells, animals, and retinue prospered and enlarged, he had to leave Gerar. He left peaceably, but far too often the ancient Hebrew praised God for helping his tribe take over another peoples' land.

The slaughter of tribes who worshipped alien gods, slaughter commanded by God, disturbs me. In Psalm 44, we read:

We have heard with our ears, O God, our fathers have told us
What you did in their time,

*How you drove out the heathen with your hand, and planted
    our fathers in,*
*How you destroyed the nations, and made your own people
    to flourish,*
*For they did not get the land in possession through their
    own sword,*
neither was it their own arm that helped them,
*But your right hand, and your arm, and the light of your
    countenance,*
because you favoured them.
You are my King, O God,
send help to Jacob.
Through you we will overthrow our enemies,
*and in your name we will tread under those who rise up
    against us.*

This triumphalism is profoundly disturbing. But Scripture makes it clear that we are never to stay in one place, one way of thinking, but to move on, out into the wilderness, as El Shaddai moved Abraham, Isaac, and Jacob. As promised, they had many descendants and, alas, a large population seems to encourage war.

But on a planet where population has grown beyond bounds, this warring way of life does not work any more. Wars in the name of religion not only give religion a bad name, they are a warning that it is time for us to move out of and beyond the old tribalism. Not easy, for it would seem that some form of tribalism is inherent in human nature. Science fiction writers often cast their characters in the old tribal mode, even when the tribe is the people of this planet, and the neighbours, "them," are from other planets. In Star Trek, the tribe includes a Martian, so "us" is the solar system, and "them" (usually the bad guys) are from other solar systems. Sometimes it is this galaxy that is the tribe, versus other galaxies.

But everything we are learning about the nature of Being is making it apparent that "us" versus "them" is a violation of Creation. Tribalism must be transformed into community. We are learning from astrophysics and particle physics and cellular biology that all of Creation exists only in interdependence and unity.

In a recent article on astrophysics I came across the beautiful and imaginative concept known as "the butterfly effect." If a butterfly winging over the fields around Crosswicks should be hurt, the effect would be felt in galaxies thousands of light years away. The interrelationship of all of Creation is sensitive in a way we are just beginning to understand. If a butterfly is hurt, we are hurt. If the bell tolls, it tolls for us. We can no longer even think of saying, "In the Name of the Lord will I destroy them." No wonder Jesus could say that not one sparrow could fall to the ground without the Father's knowledge.

Dr. Paul Brand points out that every cell in the body has its own specific job, in interdependence with every other cell. The only cells which insist on being independent and autonomous are cancer cells.

Surely that should be a lesson to us in the churches. Separation from each other, and from the rest of the world is not only disaster for us, but for everybody from whom we separate ourselves. We must be very careful lest in insisting on our independence we become malignant.

If we take the whole sweep of the story, rather than isolating passages out of context, this is the message of Scripture. So now, as we take the next steps into the wilderness into which God is sending us; now, as the human creature has moved from being the primitive hunter to the land-worker to the city-dweller to the traveller in the skies, we must move on to a way of life where we are so much God's one people that warfare is no longer even a possibility. It is that, or dis-aster, and we must not let Satan, the great separator, win.

The phrase, "the butterfly effect," comes from the language of physics. It is equally the language of poetry, and of theology. For the Christian, the butterfly has long been a symbol of resurrection.

The butterfly emerges from the cocoon, its wings, wet with rebirth, slowly opening, and then this creature of fragile loveliness flies across the blue vault of sky.

Butterflies and angels, seraphim and cherubim, call us earthbound creatures to lift up our mortal dust and sing with them, to God's delight.

Holy. Holy. Holy!

Let the Floods Clap Their Hands

3

ESAU WAS A MORE PRIMITIVE personality than Jacob. He lived for the moment, with little thought of the morrow, or the consequences of his impulses. When he came home from hunting, famished, and saw that Jacob had made pottage (a delicious stew of rice, lentils, and onions), the smell was too much for him, and he asked Jacob to give him a bowlful.

Jacob's response was hardly generous—surely he could have shared with Esau! But, no; he demanded Esau's birthright as the price of a mess of pottage. Because Esau was famished and because that moment was all he was thinking about, he let Jacob trick him, and to fill his immediate need he thoughtlessly gave away his birthright as eldest son. While this was merely imprudent of Esau, it was a thoroughly dirty trick on Jacob's part; but Jacob never hesitated to pull dirty tricks. And yet it was Jacob, not Esau, who became the third person in the trinity of patriarchs. Over and over in Scripture we hear the invocation: "the God of Abraham, Isaac, and Jacob." And God named Jacob *Israel*—one man as the icon of a nation.

45

Poor hairy Esau, more like a monkey than a man. Perhaps he compensated by becoming a mighty hunter, whereas Jacob, who was called to be Israel, stayed home with his mother. Jacob cooked the savoury smelling pottage Esau was so hungry for. Jacob did many things which today are considered effeminate. It is almost as much of a shock to us to think of Jacob staying around the tent, cooking rice, onions, and lentils, as it is for us to visualize Jesus eating at Matthew's house with all those sinful people. Jacob, in a masculine world, had feminine qualities, and so, despite his cheating, he also had intuition and a willing suspension of disbelief.

Take a new look, these unexpected happenings seem to say. Jacob may not be who you thought he was. You may not be who you think you are, or who you think you ought to be.

The glorious message of Scripture is that we do not have to be perfect for our Maker to love us. All through the great stories, heavenly love is lavished on visibly imperfect people. Scripture asks us to look at Jacob as he really is, to look at ourselves as we really are, and then realize that this is who God loves. God did not love Jacob because he was a cheat, but because he was Jacob. God loves us in our complex *is*ness, and when we get stuck on the image of the totally virtuous and morally perfect person we will never be, we are unable to accept this unqualified love, or to love other people in their rich complexity.

If God can love Jacob—or any single one of us—as we really are, then it is possible for us to turn in love to those who hurt or confuse us. Those we know and those we do not know. And that makes me take a new look at love.

It is not easy. The forensic attitude is deeply engrained. I need the help of the Holy Spirit in order to turn my demands for fairness to love, as (for instance) when I think about whoever it was who was willing to allow me to take the blame for something I did not do. It is not easy to reject the forensic response, but it is essential. And does it make any difference if I try to think of those two horrid men on my jury duty case with love? If the world and all of us in it are as interdependent as the physicists tell us, yes. If the butterfly effect is true, yes, it does make a difference. They don't have to be perfect, or even repentant, to be loved. Of course they won't ever know that I am trying to love them, but that does not negate love. Not if it is part of the love of God.

And Jacob received the beneficence of that love.

Why Jacob?

The stories of the great scriptural characters are not stories about fairness. Life is not fair. Indeed, the idea of fairness and unfairness didn't come into being until after the Fall. In Eden there was no need to think about such things, because life was the joy of at-one-ment with the Creator. It is after the fracture of this union, this separation (the first apartheid), that we begin to get caught up in shoulds and oughts, and fair and unfair. Children tend to stamp their feet and cry out, "It's not fair!" and very likely it isn't. When we think in terms of fairness and unfairness, we begin to want to "pay back" whoever has been unfair, we begin to want to get even, to punish. That is the beginning of forensic thinking.

Unfortunately, as many of us move on in chronology, we tend to stay stuck in the "It's not fair!" frame of mind, which, for the adult, is crippling. It takes great courage to live in a world where fairness simply doesn't play a part, and hasn't, since Adam and Eve ate of the fruit of the tree of the knowledge of good and evil. And one of Satan's most successful ploys is his insistence that things ought to be fair. The good should be rewarded; the bad should be punished. If we think forensically and earn enough merit badges everything will work out just as we would like. But that is not how grace works.

In a fair world, that tornado which devastated our trees would have gone some place where people didn't lovingly tend the land. But tornadoes don't have anything to do with fairness. It is easier to understand that the "natural" world operates on principles where fairness plays no part than it is to understand that we cannot dwell overmuch on fairness with human nature, either. In a fair world no child would be struck down by a drunken driver; no family would have to grieve; no one would have to carry the burden of killing. In a fair world there would be no crime, no violence in the streets, no body cells growing out of control with cancer. Fairness is devoutly to be desired, but it is not the way things are. In this world the wicked flourish and the innocent suffer, and the Lord of all is no respecter of persons, and may sometimes speak through the wicked even more clearly than through the innocent.

In our own cumbersome, unwieldly court system, which is nevertheless one of the better court systems in the world, those who can afford the best lawyers are more likely to be given a verdict of Not Guilty than those who have to take whatever lawyer the state assigns them. During my time on jury duty in January, I was very aware that the two arrogant men had managed to retain very clever lawyers, who were doing their best to clear them, according to the law, whether or not they believed them to be guilty of the crime of which they were accused. We jurors were not at all sure that justice was going to prevail.

And in my own life I was struggling to accept the fact that justice was not going to be done. I did *not* have to be exonerated over that spilled secret. I did *not* have to know who told, and then allowed me to be blamed. I had to let go thoughts of justice and vindication, and live with the situation as it was, as lovingly as possible. Which was not very.

Why is it so hard to understand that in this world everything is not going to turn out all right, all strings neatly tied, and justice triumphant? If we take the short view, it would be almost impossible not to drop into pessimism. It is not easy, in the midst of tragedy or trauma, to take the long view, to understand that ultimately there is meaning, meaning we may not in our lifetimes ever understand.

It is impossible for us finite creatures to understand the infinite Author of All in any definitive way. We can never say, This is God, Q.E.D. We would like to feel that we understand God, and the Creator's ways, but we can't. We never have. Not since the Garden. The important message, throughout Scripture, is that God understands us and loves us, and so frees us to keep our concept of el open to change as revelation comes to us in new and unexpected ways.

When Jacob tricked his twin brother, Esau was justly out-raged. Outrage is an emotion we are all familiar with. When something horrendous happens we want the perpetrator of the crime to be punished. We look for justice, absolute justice, rather than mercy. The Psalms are full of outrage and demands for redress:

Let my adversaries be clothed with shame, and let them cover themselves with their own confusion, as with a cloak . . . Break their teeth, O God, in their mouths, smite the jawbones of the lions, O Lord. Let them fall away like running water; when they shoot their arrows, let them be rooted out. Let them slime away like a snail, and be like the untimely fruit of a woman, and let them not see the sun. Or ever your pots be made hot with thorns, he shall take them away with a whirlwind, the green and burning alike. The righteous shall rejoice when he sees vengeance, he shall wash his footsteps in the blood of the ungodly.

No!
Not any more.
Now we have to move beyond that.

Am I only like my dog with her rawhide bone, chewing and chewing until there is nothing left? It has been pointed out to me that this vengeance against enemies was obedience to the

Lord, and that this obedience is the highest law. But is it? Didn't Jesus break the Mosaic law in order to obey the higher law of love?

It takes more maturity than many of us possess to want the monstrous criminal to repent, saying to God and to us, "Forgive me. I am horrified at what I have done. I am sorry, sorry, and I will never do it again. With your help I will turn my life to love."

Hate the sin and love the sinner is too easy. As long as there is any hate in us we are not ready for heaven, not as long as we're shutting the golden doors on anyone else.

I continued my own struggle during that time on jury duty. Several evenings, when I was tired and wanted to relax, I received angry phone calls from people condemning me for telling that terrible secret I had not told. All I could say was that I had not breathed a word. Some people believed me. Some did not. It is a taint in human nature to like to see someone else do wrong so that we can affirm our own righteousness. My own wish to find out who had told the secret was a part of this taint. I was well aware that, as my friend Tallis points out, we cannot afford the luxury of hurt feelings. My head could get that all straight, but there was still hurt in my heart.

I thought of the heavenly banquet, where part of my job might have to be blowing up the balloons and setting the place for whoever it was who willingly dumped blame on me—a job which would have to be done, ultimately, with love. Not just forgiveness, but love. And I knew I wasn't ready, yet. And what was going on in the courtroom during the day helped me to see the situation more clearly than otherwise might have been possible.

But it still hurt.

And I had to let that hurt go. I could not hold on to it.

Ernest L. Boyer, Jr., in *A Way in the World*, writes, "Forgiveness is, then, a renewal, and for love to grow it must be renewed every day. This renewal is not one that seeks somehow to return to the past, however; rather, it seeks to revitalize the present. To carry a grudge is to live in the past, to live with the bitterness of disappointment of the expectation of a future that never was."

To carry a grudge is to live in the past. That hit home. It helped me to move into the present so that there might be hope for friendship to be reborn.

Boyer continues, "Both of these—the past that is now gone and the future that never was—are illusionary worlds. Forgiveness frees a person to live in the reality of the relationship's present."

Esau has something to teach us here. He was willing to sell his birthright to satisfy his immediate desire for food, but he did not carry grudges. He did not live in the past. He had no expectations of impossible futures. Once his anger at Jacob was spent, he did not dwell on it. He let it go.

The two men who were being tried for assault in the second degree struck me as grudge keepers. Shouldn't that have taught me something?

The heavenly banquet cannot begin until we are all there, and I can greet with love the two resentful men, and everybody who has caused me pain, and call out a welcome to them all. The heavenly banquet cannot begin until all those whom I have hurt are ready to welcome me, in all my flawed and contradictory humanness.

Forgiveness which leads to welcoming, with open arms, the forgiven ones to the party, comes less from an act of will than from a gift of grace. Sometimes prayer opens the door to this gift.

Prayer is most real when it moves away from forensic demands, from a crime and punishment, eye-for-an-eye thinking, and into an open and vulnerable listening. It is not so much talking to God as being quiet and focussing on listening, so that perhaps we will be able to hear if God has something to say.

When I was a little girl I used to say my prayers, ending, "and God bless me and make me a good girl." As I grow older,

I become less and less sure that it was a good prayer, as I become less and less sure what being a good girl actually meant.

I suppose in my case it meant that I was to honour my mother and father, and I can't fault that. It meant that I was to obey them which, as long as I was a child—accepting everything from them, food, clothing, housing, ideas, schooling—was right and proper, especially since they were reasonable and loving parents. It also meant that I was not to tell lies. That I was to keep clean. That I was to be courteous. To be considerate of other people.

So what's wrong with it?

Did it imply that being a "good girl" was in my control? Did it imply a degree of conscious direction of my feelings and actions which life has taught me that I don't have?

Sure, I want to be "good," but can I consider myself "good" in a world where a small proportion of the people have too much to eat while the rest of the world is starving? Where a small proportion of us live comfortably if not luxuriously, while the rest of the world is in favelas and barrios and ghettos or out on the streets? Can I closet myself in my "goodness" while there is injustice and prejudice and terrorism?

Perhaps I may not personally cheat the government, consider the poor expendable, murder, steal, mug, or rape. Perhaps I may not use a knife with the intent to injure or kill. Perhaps I try to eat a diet suitable for a small planet. But can I separate my own health from the rest of the world? my own good nutrition from the poor nutrition of billions? my longing for peace from the warring in the Middle East or South America or Ireland or anywhere else at all? In a universe where the lifting of the wings of a butterfly is felt across galaxies, I cannot isolate myself, because my separation may add to the starvation and the anger and the violence.

I am not burdening myself with a lot of guilts which are impossible for me to resolve. But to separate myself from the suffering of the world is dis-aster. If I call myself "good" is that not separation?

Jesus said, "Why do you call me good? Only my father is good."

Aren't we supposed to be good? Do we always have the wisdom to know what good is? If we truly understand what Jesus was saying, we know that what matters is not moralism, but understanding that God with infinite grace can work goodness through us. Goodness is of God; we cannot make ourselves good through an act of will.

Surely the Inquisitors thought they were being good, that they were doing God's will, when they tortured people (whether innocent or guilty is hardly the point). Terrorists think that they are being good, nay, holy, when they throw bombs and shoot guns in religious zeal. Those in South Africa who believe in apartheid think they are being good when they assume they are superior to any one of another colour.

Trying, of our own virtue, to be good, usually leads to disaster. If I, self-consciously, try to make myself good, I am unwittingly separating myself from those I love and would serve.

I learned this the hard way during our four summers of four generations living together under one not very large roof. I wouldn't have missed those summers. They were a kind of miracle in this day and age, and I have written about them in *A Circle of Quiet* and *The Summer of the Great Grandmother.* I learned that if I tried to be good, that is, if I tried to be the perfect wife, mother, daughter, grandmother, all I did was become exhausted and ill and humourless and help nobody. If I spent the morning at the typewriter; if, in the late afternoon before I cooked dinner, I went off with the dogs for a walk, the entire household was happier, there was more laughter and song. I learned that if I was what I had considered selfish, that is, if I took reasonable care of my own needs, we had a smoothly running household. Paradox, as always.

If I am ever good, it is not because I am trying to be, but because goodness is for a moment offered me as a gift of sheer grace. Jesus made it very clear that goodness comes from God, not from el's creatures.

Not that I want to wallow in my own sin and badness, or that I see myself as hated by God because I am human and often do wrong. Actions have consequences, but that is not what "original sin" means, and we need to rethink "original sin" just as much as we needed to rethink the impassible God who could not suffer. Does any mother, holding her newborn babe in her arms, see anything except innocence and purity and God's delight?

How did we get hung up on "goodness" as a criterion? If that were so, God would not have called Abraham, or Isaac, or Jacob. Especially not Jacob. It is quite clear that Jacob was not "good."

Nor was he particularly religious; he was slow to accept the God of his fathers. But even before he had decided to call their God his God, too, he made altars, upon which he poured sacred oil. How many altars Jacob made! One day I'll count them, but I'm less interested in adding up numbers than in the need to make altars, to understand sacred spaces.

I, too, have my altars, such as the Star Watching Rock and the Icon Tree. Whether we acknowledge it or not, we all have our own altars (and a kitchen stove on which meals are cooked with love is not an unworthy one), altars which may be for us ladders of angels, joining heaven and earth, God and creature.

* * *

In this time of increasing stress and tension we need our altars of affirmation, our ladders drawing us to adoring awe.

Not easy. If, twenty-five years ago, I had somehow been allowed to see a few clips from almost any evening's news, I'd have found it impossible to believe. We've had assassinations, scandals, bombings, kidnappings, hijackings, and crisis after crisis among nations.

In my own neighbourhood in New York, in twenty-five years I've seen stores previously only locked at night now protected with iron gates to keep out vandals. Private guards help the city police to patrol the streets. Not long ago my husband put me in a taxi to go downtown to give a talk, and told me to put my gold earrings in my pocket till I arrived, commenting, "Isn't this a terrible way to live."

He was not being an alarmist. Only a few days before, a friend of ours had been walking along Broadway past Lincoln Center, when she felt an arm go about her neck—and her gold chain was gone. She said the thief must have been extremely professional, because she could not find a mark on her neck.

What has happened to our country in the past quarter-of-a-century would be incomprehensible to my grandparents, but it has all happened and is happening. We need to be aware of it, and to try to listen to God for what our part is in trying to change it, to bring terrorism to compassion, greed to generosity, lust to love. We don't have to succeed, single-handedly, in reforming the world, or in improving the morals of those around us by our own goodness. God-Within-Us-In-Jesus did none of these things.

But if we listen, we will be given the courage to do whatever it is that God wants us to do, big things or, more likely, small. This faith in God's gifts of courage and grace is like a foundation of rock under my feet, even as I help pile the wood from the trees ripped off at their roots by the twister, even as the bed shakes under me in the earthquake, even as I take the crowded rush hour subway down to Manhattan's criminal court.

* ❋ *

How can we expect peace in the world, sanity in our cities, when as Christians we cannot live creatively together with all our wonderfully diverse ways of affirming our love of God? Why are we so concerned about those who do not express their faith in exactly the same way that we do? If I need a doctor, I am not going to ask, "What is your denomination?" any more than I am going to inquire about sexual preference. What I want to know is: Is this a good doctor? Will I be treated effectively? Can I be cured?

When we worry about someone's denomination, we sometimes forget that this person may be a superb surgeon, or pianist, or car mechanic. We sometimes forget that our own vocations are not limited by denominational boundaries. Our responsibility as faithful people of God is in every area of our lives, not only in our church-going.

If I am true in my living to what I proclaim in my writing it is because of grace, not virtue. It has little to do with my denomination. I pray for grace, knowing that it is not mine to grasp; it is a gift of love.

And of course I am not always true to what I proclaim. I am human and flawed and frequently fall flat on my face. All of us do, even the saints. But we struggle to be true. If we struggle honestly, humbly, the angels will help us.

When they do, it is usually when we least expect it, when we have to respond to something or someone immediately, and so don't have time to get ourselves in the way. I turned from the typewriter to answer the phone, and it was a young woman in Oregon. We'd met at a writer's conference, and corresponded sporadically. She's lively and bright and talented.

Her question came at me out of the blue. "Madeleine—all the things you've written, do you believe them?"

"Yes, I do."

"You really do?"

"If I didn't believe them, I couldn't survive."

"I'm in the hospital. I had a hysterectomy. I can't ever have a baby."

To a young woman in her twenties this is a bitter blow. What she had expected to be a simple D and C (though she'd signed the release for further surgery if necessary) had revealed a malignancy.

"The doctor says the outlook is good, but he wants me to have chemotherapy, anyhow. Oh, God, Madeleine, I try not to say, *Why did this happen to me*—" She started to cry.

I wanted to put my arms around her and hold her, and did the best I could, long distance.

When she had stopped crying, she said, "I don't know why I had to call you and tell you all my troubles. I just need to be sure you believe what you say in your books."

"I do." God help me, I do. Even when I don't, I do.

(And that is the truth: even when I don't, I do.)

"You'll pray for me?"

"Of course." This means simply holding this young woman out (or in) to God's love, and visualizing her as whole and healthy and beautiful.

The important thing about this conversation was that I was given the grace of affirming all that my books say at a time when that affirmation was needed. And not only by my young friend, by me, too.

Now, this young woman was not in any conservative sense of the word, a "practicing Christian." But she asked for prayers, and that was enough, more than enough.

Jesus did not limit his love to those accepted by the establishment. He spoke with Samaritans, even making a Samaritan woman the protagonist of one of his parables, despite the fact that the Samaritans were the socially despised, the religiously untouchable. In that culture one didn't take water from a *woman* in the casual way that Jesus did, and even less from a Samaritan woman. But he did.

If we Christians truly love one another, that love spreads out to include all the Samaritans and the Canaanites and unbelievers and worshippers of Baal and the unorthodox and the heterodox and even the Shiites and Khomeini and Idi Amin and Muammar Qaddafi—and the two men on trial in criminal court.

Perhaps we have been giving too many answers instead of asking questions, of ourselves, of each other, of God. Montaigne's "Que sais-je?" sits more comfortably with me than Descartes' "Je pense, donc je suis."

The most brilliant people really don't know very much. We will not move along on our journey if we are afraid to ask questions. What is my place in this glorious universe? Where shall I set my stone pillow to make an altar? Will there be a ram? Or a butterfly? What do you want me to do? How can I criticize less and love more? How can I show in my own life the loveliness of creativity? Can I call a Christian from another denomination less Christian than those in my own without further battering the broken bride of Christ? How do I help to heal and not to separate?

Never with pride. Never with being sure that I am right and everybody else is wrong.

There's an old story of a student who went to a famous old rabbi and said, "Master, in the old days there were people who could see God. Why is it that nobody sees God nowadays?"

The old man answered, "My child, nowadays nobody can stoop so low."

$$* \text{ } * \text{ } *$$

Why are we afraid of stooping so low? Didn't the second person of the Trinity stoop lower than we can even conceive when he willingly relinquished all power and glory to come to earth as a human baby?

We find it difficult to understand that the magnificence and might of all Creation is also small and vulnerable. Isn't the Creator supposed to be invulnerable? Isn't that what used to be taught in seminary? If God can be hurt, what kind of protection can this suffering servant give us?

But God, in choosing to become incarnate, with all our human limitations, also chose the possibility of being hurt. Possibility? Probability? Inevitability? Those who are fully alive are also usually those who have been deeply wounded, and the God who came to us in Jesus of Nazareth was fully alive, with an awareness and a joy and a perceptiveness most of us can only wonder at. Along with the joy was a willingness to assume all of our human sufferings, which should make us look differently at our own pain.

Would I really be able to worship a God who was simply implacable power, and who was invulnerable? If I am hurt, I don't turn for strength and help to someone who has never been hurt, but to someone who has, and who can therefore understand a little of what I am going through. The people I know who are the most invulnerable also tend to show the least compassion.

The kind of person I turn to is someone who has been strong enough to face pain when it comes—and it does come. Someone who faces it, endures it, and tries as hard as possible to go through it and come out on the other side. Someone whose urge for health is strong enough to hold on to wholeness even in the midst of suffering. And someone who manages to retain a sense of humour, who has the gift of laughter.

As these are the qualities I look for in another human being when I am in need of healing, so these are the qualities I look for in God.

And it is God who promises the Heavenly Banquet, the banquet which is for all of creation, for every single one of us, all us members of the jury, the two arrogant defendants, and their clever lawyers. We will all be changed in the twinkling of an eye (though that may be many thousands of years in human time), come to ourselves, even if it brings us bitter tears of self-revelation before we can turn to love.

To be in a state of unforgiveness is to know hell, at least in a small way. I know, because I've been there. It's not easy to get out of hell, but it can be done, when we come to ourselves and turn to the source of all love.

Belief in hell is lack of faith, Berdyaev said to me in his book as I sat in the jury room. "Belief in hell is lack of faith because it is to attribute more power to Satan than to God."

I know what Berdyaev was trying to say. He was emphasizing Satan's ultimate downfall. In the meantime hell remains to be conquered. I believe in hell, but my faith in the power of Satan and the fallen angels is nowhere near as strong as my belief in the eternal and infinite power of the Creator. Paul, in his first letter to the Corinthians, asks, "O death, where is thy sting? O grave, where is thy victory?" But then he makes a marvellous affirmation—"Thanks be to God, who gives us the victory through our Lord Jesus Christ!" Though Satan cannot win the final victory, during our lifetimes we will all experience the sting of death, the dark power of hell and the grave. But it is not the last word. It is God who has the last word!

We are all going to face God's judgment, but we will not receive forensic judgment from the throne of heaven. Listen to the way judgment is referred to in these lines from the 98th Psalm:

Show yourselves joyful in the Lord, all you lands,
sing, rejoice, and give thanks.

Praise the Lord upon the harp, sing to the harp
with a psalm of thanksgiving.

With trumpets, and with horns, O show yourselves
joyful before the Lord, the King.

Let the sea make a noise and all that is in it;
the round world and all that dwell on it.

Let the floods clap their hands, and let the hills
be joyful together before the Lord,
for he is come to judge the earth,

With righteousness shall he judge the world
and the peoples with his truth.

That sounds more as though we were preparing for a celebration than judgment, but isn't that what judgment is really about? For the judgment of God does not falter. God is not going to abandon Creation, nor the people up for trial in criminal court, nor the Shiites nor the communists nor the warmongers, nor the greedy and corrupt people in high places, nor the dope pushers, nor you, nor me. Bitter tears of repentance may be shed before we can join the celebration, but it won't be complete until we are all there.

The book of the prophet, Micah, ends with these words:

Who is a God like you, who pardons iniquity, and overlooks the transgressions of us all. He does not hold on to his anger, because he delights in mercy. He will have pity on us, and will subdue our faults, and will cast all our sins into the depths of the sea. Grant Jacob your truth, and your mercy to Abraham, as you promised to our forbears from the days of old.

This is the God of Scripture, the God of forbearance, forgiveness, and unqualified love. We have been living in a world where we have viewed God and each other in a forensic way for too long, and it should be apparent that it is not working, and that it is not going to work. This forensic world is not a scriptural world, but a clever projection of the Tempter. It is not helping our traffic jams. It will not help the national debt. It will not help our peacemakers to keep the peace. Our planet totters on the brink of disaster. Our only hope for peace, within our own hearts, and all over our small green earth, is for us to open ourselves to the judgment of God, that judgment that makes the waters and the hills to sing. For God's judgment is atonement, at-one-ment, making us one with the Lord of love.

> *Let the floods clap their hands, and let the hills*
> *be joyful together before the Lord,*
> *for he is come to judge the earth,*
> *with righteousness shall he judge the world*
> *and the peoples with his truth.*

What Are You Looking For?

4

WHEN I WAS A CHILD nobody told me that I should read the Bible piously, so I read it just as I read Hans Christian Andersen and George MacDonald and books of fairy tales. I read it as story, great story, about fascinating and complex people called by God to do amazing things.

Perhaps it was a blessing that as a child I was not taken to Sunday school. I have met far too many people who have had to spend years in the difficult task of unlearning bad Sunday school teaching, who have found it almost impossible to get rid of the image of an angry God, out to punish them.

My church teaches that the Bible contains everything necessary for salvation. What on earth do we mean by that?

I can affirm it only if I know what the Bible is, and what it is not. It is a living book, not a dead one. It urges us to go beyond its pages, not to stop with what we have read. It is a book not only of history, and of the prohibitions of the commandments and laws, but of poetry and song, of fantasy and paradox and mystery and contradiction.

It is not the only book in which I will look for and find truth. There is much to inspire me, to widen my understanding of the Creator, in the works of Shakespeare, Dante, Dostoyevsky. There are important insights into the nature of God in the sacred books of other religions. When I was a child, my parents had these words framed and hung in the bathroom:

Listen to the exhortation of the dawn.
Look to this day, for it is life, the very life of life.
In its brief course lie all the verities and realities
  of your existence,
the glory of action—the bliss of growth
  the splendour of beauty.
For yesterday is but a dream,
and tomorrow is only a vision,
but today, well lived,
makes every yesterday a dream of happiness,
and every tomorrow a vision of hope.
Look well therefore to this day.
Such is the salutation of the dawn.

Good words, those, good words to live by. They come from the Koran. Does that mean that my Episcopalian parents were flirting with Islam? Of course not. I've memorized those words, because they help keep me aware of the wonders of each day, even when they may be painful.

Hugh and I spent seven hours in the emergency room of a big New York hospital, a scene of pain, noise, fear, confusion. Hugh woke up with a pain in the chest. Our doctor was away for the weekend (of course this was Saturday), so it was off to the emergency room. Seven hours, mostly spent waiting, once the electrocardiogram was normal. But then there were hours spent facing the possibility that the pain might be from a pulmonary embolism. And at last, at the seventh hour, the welcome news that it was from pulled muscles, with perhaps a cracked rib, from the strain of trying to open one of the recalcitrant, ancient windows in our apartment. Oh, the joy of sitting down together at our own table, an hour after Hugh was released, to eat dinner together! The joy in the simple ordinariness of a simple meal in our own home! Indeed, look well therefore to this day.

It is not only in the religious writings of various peoples that I find truth. I find that my forbearance is widened, my understanding of human potential expanded, as I read fiction, even if it is only to disagree with a narrow or ugly view of life, or to turn away from discontent. The fiction to which I turn and return is that which has a noble understanding of God's purpose for all that has been created.

My theology is deepened and broadened as I study the new sciences. I do try to read with discrimination, to turn to writers whose vision is not mean or narrow or degrading. It was a sad moment when I had to admit to myself that I was not going to be able to read, in this lifetime, all the books I need to read!

I turn daily to the Bible because in it are the stories of my own tradition, of what Jung calls our racial memory. The story of Jacob is my story, too.

Karl Barth said, "I take the Bible far too seriously to take it literally." The Bible is a book which urges us to keep our concept of God open, to let our understanding grow and develop as we are illumined by new discoveries. If we stopped where Scripture leaves us, in the New Testament as well as the Old, we could still, with clear consciences, keep slaves. The apostle Paul exhorts masters to treat their slaves well, and slaves to be obedient, with no hint that slave-owning may not be a good thing in the eyes of God. According to the law, a woman taken in adultery was to be stoned. To death. Not men. If we stopped, literally, with Scripture, we could keep on justifying going into any country we wanted, when we needed extra living space, and slaughtering the heathen natives, because God is on our side, and will help get rid of the pagans for us, so we can have their country.

Who are the pagans? A child, asked this question in Sunday school, replied, "The pagans are the people that don't quarrel about God."

It is terrifying to realize that we can prove almost anything we want to prove if we take fragments of the Bible out of context. Those who believe in the righteousness of apartheid believe that this is scriptural. I turn to the Bible in fear and trembling, trying to see it whole, not using it for my own purposes, but letting its ongoing message of love direct me.

The problem of extra living space for an over-crowded planet is one with which science fiction writers have honestly struggled in their depiction of space exploration, with few answers. The old legalism was, perhaps, behind the way the pioneers treated the Indians—not all the pioneers, thank God, but some of them. Did they justify giving the Indians blankets impregnated with smallpox virus because they knew God wanted the white man, not the heathen, to have the land?

Scriptural literalism has caused and still causes incredible damage. But I don't want to throw up my hands and toss out Scripture because we have constantly misused it.

How do those of us who are not seminary students or theologians read the Book creatively and not destructively? Not, I think, with volumes of interpretation—not, that is, for our daily reading. We must take it as it is. What a passage says to us today may not be what the same passage will say when we next encounter it. We must strive to be open to the deeply mythic quality, expressing the longings and aspirations and searchings of the human race.

After a tiring day on jury duty I sat in my quiet corner and picked up the Bible. In Matthew's gospel, I turned to chapter 11 where Jesus was speaking to the multitudes about his cousin, John. He asked,

> "What did you go out into the wilderness to see? A reed shaken in the wind? But what did you look for? A man clothed in soft raiment? Look, they that wear soft raiment are found in king's houses. But what did you look for? a prophet? yes, a prophet indeed, and more than a prophet."

And he continued, asking the people,

> "What is this generation like? It is like children sitting in the market place, and calling to their companions, saying we have piped for you, and you have not danced, we have mourned for you, and you have not grieved." John came, neither eating, nor drinking and the people accused him of having a devil. And the Son of man came eating and drinking, and they accused him of being gluttonous, and a wine bibber, and a friend of publicans and sinners."

"What are you looking for?" Jesus asked the people.

What are we looking for? Are we looking for things we can criticize, or are we looking for Christ, for love and compassion? Are we looking for evidence that our Christian group is *the* group, with *the* truth, or are we looking for at-one-ment?

I care very much about Christian unity, and therefore it gives me great joy when I am privileged to speak with many different kinds of Christian groups. I had the pleasure of being the keynote speaker in Boston at a gathering of two thousand United Methodist women. Shortly thereafter I had the joy of receiving an honorary doctorate from Wheaton College, in Illinois, and from there I went to Dallas, Texas, to teach at a Christian Writers Conference. Following that, I preached at the

Episcopal Cathedral Church of St. John the Divine in New York; on to Immanuel Congregational Church (United Church of Christ) in Hartford, Connecticut. Back to Boston for the Catholic Library Association, and on, the next weekend, to Presbyterian Wilson College in Pennsylvania. I came home from all this ecumenical travelling, and I said, fervently, to my husband, "I've had it with Christians."

How could I possibly say such a thing?

Not because of the majority of loving, faithful people I met, but because of a minority, small, but growing, of people who seemed to think they were called to discover the devil in other people. (Believe me, when you look for the devil, you'll find him.)

Jesus was accused of casting out devils by the Devil. He was

casting out a devil, and it was dumb. And when the devil was gone out of the man, he was able to speak. And some of the people said, "He casts out devils through Beelzebub, the chief of devils." Jesus answered them, "Every kingdom divided against itself will fall. If Satan is divided against himself, how can his kingdom stand? You say that I cast out devils through the devil, well, if I cast out devils by the devil, by whom do your sons cast them out? They will be your judges. But if I, with the finger of God, cast out devils, then the kingdom of God is come upon you."

What are we looking for?

The people who accused Jesus of casting out devils by the Devil frighten me. The people who are looking to see if they can accuse someone of being in league with the Devil frighten me, too. There aren't many of them, yet, but I met or heard one or two every place I went. They are powerful, and they claim to be Christians, to be even better Christians than those of us who are looking for Christ, for love, rather than Satan.

And they are dividing the kingdom, and Jesus warns that a

kingdom divided against itself will fall.

There are times when I may have had it with Christians, but I do not want the kingdom to fall. My hope and my faith is that we can worship God in our different ways, and still be one body. My feet walk, my eyes see, my nose smells, but I am still one body. And that one body is a part of the body of Christ.

As Christians, we have a responsibility to love one another, not to be suspicious and judgmental. The early Christians were not divided into inimical factions. Jesus Christ, and him crucified, and risen from the dead, was what mattered. Anyone looking at the divided body of Christ today might be tempted to imagine Jesus gathering the disciples together and saying, "Hey, Peter, you start the Roman Catholic Church. John, why don't you get the Episcopalians going? James, do you want the Baptists? Andrew, what about Methodism? Philip, can you start the Presbyterians?"

Is that the kind of body of Christ Scripture talks about? How can we have an effective evangelism if we are a divided body? How can we even call ourselves Christian?

Many years ago I belonged to a group which put on a musical comedy each spring, the proceeds going to the two churches in the village—I won't bother to mention what denomination they were. One year the regular director was away, and I was asked to take over. I didn't want to immerse myself for several months in music I might get tired of, so with incredible naiveté and a notable lack of common sense, I decided that we would do Smetana's *The Bartered Bride*. *The Bartered Bride*, I discovered to my rue, is no musical comedy. It is not even an operetta. It is an opera. Eventually we came up with an excellent production, but I was totally exhausted, and those of us involved called it not the *Bartered* Bride, but the *Battered* Bride.

That's us, the Christian church right now, the Battered Bride. We are supposed to be the bride of Christ, but what kind of bride are we? Not very beautiful.

The terrible difference between us, the bride of Christ, and the tragic brides who are beaten by their husbands, is that it is we, ourselves, who are doing the battering. With our warring denominations we have scratched at each others' eyes, pummeled and punched each other and ourselves, and so disgraced our host. What kind of a bruised and bloodied face do we show to the world? What kind of a bride of Christ do we make visible?

We will not become beautiful again until religion becomes a unifying and not a divisive word. We will not be beautiful again until we look for love, rather than Satan. We do find what we look for.

A letter came to me from a woman who was in charge of taking photographs for a conference where I had recently been a speaker. She asked me if I had a picture I could send her; the snapshot she had taken of me was not usable because I was surrounded by an aura of light which, she wrote, was surely a mark of the presence of the Holy Spirit. And then she continued, sadly, that she had mentioned this to a friend, and the friend's response had been that perhaps I was worshipping Satan, and that was what had caused the light.

Such a reaction saddens me. And frightens me. Because we do find what we look for.

As to the picture of me, it was taken with one of those cameras which spit the picture out at you, and we've all seen what odd tricks of light result, blue eyes turned to glaring red, for instance. Or it could have been old film. But it certainly did not indicate Satan worship.

I sent the photographer another picture, and in her response she told me that she had talked to another friend, who had laughed, and commented of the woman who had suggested I might be worshipping the devil, "Oh, she's on that toot, now, is she?" And my correspondent continued, "As for the tooter, I bumped into her in the supermarket the other day, and she does not look happy. Positive, but not happy."

Can one be happy while looking for Satan? I doubt it.

There's another story of light in a photograph. In Malcolm Muggeridge's book, *Something Beautiful for God,* he is writing about Mother Teresa of Calcutta. She believes that each day we should do something beautiful for God. I'm a lot happier with that than with looking for Satan. Malcolm Muggeridge describes going to one of the houses where Mother Teresa and her Sisters take care of the dying people they have rescued from the streets of Calcutta. They are tenderly nursed until they die or, in some cases, recover because of the loving care they are given. Muggeridge wanted to get a picture of the room, but Mother Teresa would not allow a flash bulb. She would not have her dying people disturbed as they were being led out of this life and into the waiting arms of Christ. Muggeridge told his photographer to take a picture anyway, without using the flash.

The photographer replied that it would be pointless; there wasn't enough light for a picture. Muggeridge said, "Take one, anyway." When the picture was developed, it had indeed taken, and the room with the cots of dying people was bathed in a lovely golden light. And that, Muggeridge felt, was a sign of the presence of the Holy Spirit. He was looking for holiness, and so he found holiness.

In *Desert Wisdom, Sayings from the Desert Fathers,* "Abba Mios was asked by a soldier whether God would forgive a sinner. After instructing him at some length, the old man asked him, 'Tell me, my dear, if your cloak were torn, would you throw it away?' 'Oh, no!' he replied. 'I would mend it and wear it again.' The old man said to him, 'Well, if you care for your cloak, will not God show mercy on his own creatures?' "

One of the desert fathers says that a dog is better than we are, because a dog loves, but does not judge. Surely that is how Doc, my golden retriever, loves me, with unqualified love, without judging me and with no expectation that I will ever be less than lovable to her. If I am judgmental of the woman who has

71

expectations of devil worship, I am falling right into the same trap she has fallen into.

One of my books was listed in a Midwestern newspaper as being pornographic. I reread the book, looking for pornography, and for the life of me could find none. Perhaps I do not know as much about pornography as the person who saw it in *A Wind in the Door.*

A beautiful letter came to me recently, in which the writer told me how much my book, *A Ring of Endless Light,* had helped her through her grief over the death of a friend. But, she said, someone had commented to her that I use swear words in the book, and how could I, as a Christian, do that?

I wrote back saying that I wasn't about to go through my book looking for swear words, but as far as I could remember, the only word in that book which might be considered a swear word is *zuggy,* a word I made up, and which means nothing, and is used by a spoiled young man who is far from being a Christian. I coined the word *zuggy,* used by that same young man, in *A Moon By Night,* in order to *avoid* using the current swear words. Somebody had to be looking very hard for swear words in order to find them. (What an ugly way to read a book!)

Even when a writer does, in fact, use such words, because they seem appropriate within the vocabulary of the character using them, searching out four-letter words is no way to read a book. A librarian friend told me of a woman who attacked *Catcher in the Rye,* a frequent target, as having in it, say, four thousand eight hundred and thirty-two swear words. "How do you know?" the librarian asked. "I counted them," the woman said. "But did you read *the book?*" "No." How sad to pick up a book looking only for dirty words and thereby perhaps missing an encounter with Christ.

Catcher in the Rye does use the language the young protagonist would use. But that is not what the book is about. It is about the loneliness of adolescence, and some of the harder lessons which must be learned in growing up, and it has helped many thoughtful youngsters to accept themselves and the world as being less perfect than we would like.

I wonder if those who search out dirty words realize that this indicates how well they know them?

What are we looking for? We should be very careful, because that is what we are going to find.

I don't want to stop being a Christian because Christians can upset and confuse me, because I fear judgmentalism in others, and also in myself, or even because sometimes in Christian settings I have seen a lack of faith in a God of love, and seen instead a God of fear and hate.

"What are you looking for?" Jesus asked.

The Gospels tell us that the professionally good people weren't looking for Jesus, and when they did, it was tentative. Nicodemus came to Jesus by night, so that he would not be seen approaching this radical teacher. Jesus was, and still is, a threat to the very establishment which proclaims him as Lord. He emphasized that he had not come to save the saved, but to save the lost, the sinners, the broken. To save the sinners, the lost, the broken, who *want* to be saved. It is possible to wallow in whatever our own particular misery is, almost taking a perverse pleasure in it. We must *want* to be healed, whole, and holy, before we can turn ourselves to Christ, and ask that we may be infused with the Spirit, and mended, so that God's image in us may become visible.

And I doubt if we can turn to Christ for healing while we are condemning anybody else.

If we, like some of the good people in Jerusalem and Nazareth and Bethlehem, are looking for people who disagree with us in order to put them down, we'll find them. If we look for people who may disagree with us, but who will challenge us to examine our own opinions and our own beliefs in a creative

*imperfections
in ourselves
in others*

73

manner, we'll find them. And we may find some wonderful surprises, as did the wounded people who flocked to Jesus.

Recently I was shown a book said to be a Christian best-seller in which the author is identifying people who worship Satan—or people she suspects of worshipping Satan. When she included Teilhard de Chardin on her list I started to laugh, then realized it was not humorous. Instead of seeing a man so in love with God that he could express his love in a book such as *The Divine Milieu,* all this author saw was a man whose view of God and Creation differed from hers. This to her was a mark of a Satan-worshipper. She also cited a fondness for unicorns as a mark of the Satan-worshipper, which is equally hilarious and frightening. The unicorn is a creature of utter purity who will approach only a true virgin of complete innocence. Since to turn towards Satan is to relinquish all innocence, is it likely that a Satan worshipper could get anywhere near a unicorn?

Do I believe in unicorns? Is a belief in a symbol of purity incompatible with belief in Christ? If so, wouldn't we have to stop having the loveliness and the family warmth of bringing in and decorating a Christmas tree, since the Christmas tree was originally a pagan practice? If a symbol leads us to a wider love of each other and of the Creator of us all, has it not in its truest sense become a Christian symbol? What would happen to my faith if I had to destroy all symbols—bread and wine, the cross?

Our faith is a faith of vulnerability and hope, not a faith of suspicion and hate. When we are looking for other people to be wrong in order that we may prove ourselves right, then we are closing ourselves off from whatever unexpected surprises Christ may be ready to offer us. If we are willing to live by Scripture, we must be willing to live by paradox and contradiction and surprise.

And what surprises! When the wonderful day of Pentecost, promised by Jesus, came, it was received with such joy that the

74

disciples were accused of being drunk although, as it was pointed out, it was only ten o'clock in the morning! We are Christians through the power of the Holy Spirit, not through our own virtue. And the Holy Spirit, is a Spirit of love and joy, not of hate and suspicion.

Witchcraft and the worship of Satan do exist. They are serious and dangerous phenomena. But when Christians look towards other Christians who worship Christ in a different manner and call them Satan-worshippers, they must please Satan. When someone accuses Teilhard de Chardin of being a Satanist, then whoever is making the accusation does not see the real Satan-worshipper who worships destruction and hate, and works for the annihilation of Christian love.

The Cathedral of St. John the Divine where I am the volunteer librarian backs onto Harlem. To the north is Columbia University. Spanish Harlem is south, and a melting pot of ethnicity to the west. One evening my friend, Canon Tallis, and I went into one of the larger chapels in the Cathedral to teach a class on preaching. There we saw pennies on the floor, arranged in the design of a pentagram. We picked them up, and I understood how my dog feels when the hair on the back of her neck prickles with apprehension.

I have been told that a chicken was found behind the altar, with its head off—a ritual, demonic blood sacrifice. I am afraid of the Satanists with their dark and secret rituals which include the shedding of blood. Sometimes, during a black mass, an infant is actually slaughtered and its blood shed. How different is this horror of shedding blood in order to appease Satan from the life-giving blood of Christ offered in the sacrament of the Eucharist. A black mass is a terrible mockery, a perverse imitation of Holy Communion, because the devil and his worshippers cannot make anything original; they can only foul and distort what God has designed with love.

As far as I know I have never met a devil worshipper (do Satanists ride the subway?) and I never want to. But I take them very seriously, and I fear them.

And I pray that we will listen to the promptings of the Holy Spirit, and not serve Satan's demonic purpose by accusing other Christians and confusing them with Satan's followers. I pray that we will learn to love one another, as the early Christians were recognized by their love, so that in all the richness of their diversity they were At One.

One of my favourite passages in John's first epistle is, "Anyone who fails to love can never have known God, because God is love. God's love for us was revealed when God sent into the world his only Son so that we could have life through him. This is the love I mean: not our love for God, but God's love for us."

It is not a simple thing to accept God's love, because if we do, we must return love. Jacob was tentative about accepting the love of his father's God, and he wanted to make sure that this tribal deity would keep his share of the bargain before he accepted him. It was not until Jacob was alone in the desert that his need overcame his wariness, and he was at last able to receive God's revelatory love.

Was it because Jacob knew himself to be a cheat and a fraud that he was able to receive the vision of God without being tempted to arrogance by it? He felt holy terror, not smugness. Self-satisfaction is what Satan offers us immediately after any manifestation of the Holy Spirit. For Satan is still a Spirit, still an angel, even if a fallen one, a negative angel eager to distort God's vision of love and turn it small and sour and selfish.

The early people of the risen Christ were not checking on other groups to see if they were less Christian than their own group, and when they did set themselves apart, Paul took them severely to task. They knew that love was what it is about, not an exclusive love, but an inclusive love, embracing all creatures, all corners of the cosmos.

When we are once more known for our love, we will be the hope of the world, and we will bear the light.

I don't want ever again to say, "I've had it with Christians," because, first of all, it isn't true. I've never *really* had it with Christians. What I'm fed up with is judgmentalness and coldness of heart. What I've had it with is those who would look for Satan, rather than Christ; who would sniff for the putrid odour of pornography rather than the lovely scent of love.

When I meet people who are truly Christian, which is often my privilege and my joy, I see people who are willing to bear the light, to *be* the light of the world—not just their own denomination's, not just the light of Christians, or of Americans, but of the world. To love where love is not easy. To bring people to Christ not through fear and coercion, but through love.

What are we looking for? The love of Christ which comes to us through the power of the Holy Spirit, that Spirit who blew in the very beginning, before there was anything at all, who spoke through the prophets, who always was, is, and will be.

Rooted
in
Cosmos
5

IN THE BEGINNING OF GENESIS, God affirms that the Creation is good—very good. The Incarnation is a reaffirmation of the innate goodness of all that God has made.

Teilhard de Chardin says that "for a soul to have a body is *enkosmismene.*"

Enkosmismene. To have our roots in the cosmos. We are like trees, drawing spiritual water through our rootedness in Creation. This is the affirmation of incarnation.

Even in time of tornado, earthquake, ice storm, our very roots are part of the entire cosmos. Surely Jacob, picking up the stone he had used for a pillow, and pouring oil on it as it became an altar, was making this same affirmation in his cry that *here* was the house of God. Jacob was indeed rooted in cosmos. At that moment he knew at-one-ment.

What actually happened to Jacob? Did God really speak to him in his dream of angels? Later, was it a physical angel who grappled with him? Is the word physical combined with angel a contradiction? Is any of this important?

As we are rooted in cosmos these images are part of the myth which the Creator gave us so that we may begin to understand something which is beyond literal interpretation by the finite human being.

On a TV interview I was asked by a clergyman if I believe that fantasy is an essential part of our understanding of the universe and our place in it, and I replied that yes, I do believe this, adding truthfully that Scripture itself is full of glorious fantasy. Yes, indeed, I take the Bible too seriously to take it all literally.

The story of Job is a wrestling with deep spiritual questions rather than dry factualism. And I love it when, in the beginning of this drama, the sons of God are gathered around, speaking to God, Satan was among them. Fallen angel or no, Satan was still God's son, and at that point was still speaking with his Creator. I wonder if he is still willing to do that, or if he has so separated himself from at-one-ment that he and his cohorts can no longer bear to be in the Presence?

And what about Ezekiel and those glorious wheels which some people think may have been U.F.O.s? There we have our first glimpse of the four horsemen of the Apocalypse. There we see the resurrection of those dry bones with living flesh, as we read the language of poetry which expands our understanding beyond its normal limitations.

The mythic interpretation is not a facile, shallow one, but an attempt to move into the deep and dazzling darkness of that truth which the fragile human mind cannot exhaustively comprehend, but can only glimpse with occasional flashes of glory.

To live with an understanding that myth is a vehicle of truth is a far more difficult way to live than literally. The mythic world makes enormous demands of us, and that may be why it is so often shunned. The greater the good we are seeking, the greater the possibilities for perversion. But that does not make God's original good any less good; it simply heightens the challenge.

I am sometimes shocked by what I read in the Bible. There is much that I am still struggling to understand, such as the horrible story in Judges of the man who divided his raped and murdered wife into twelve pieces, sending one piece to each of the tribes of Israel. I still struggle with the story of the blighted fig tree. Does it mean that when Jesus asks us to do anything, he will give us the power to do it, whether we ourselves are able to do it or not? Some of the violence in both Testaments frightens me, caught up in this age of violence. But my response of shock may be a good thing, because it pushes open doors which I might otherwise be fearful of entering.

That limited literalism which demands that the Bible's poetry and story and drama and parable be taken as factual history is one of Satan's cleverest devices. If we allow ourselves to be limited to the known and the explainable, we have thereby closed ourselves off from God and mystery and revelation.

Once I remarked that I read the Bible in much the same way that I read fairy tales, and received a shocked response. But fairy tales are not superficial stories. They spring from the depths of the human being. The world of the fairy tale is to some degree the world of the psyche. Like the heroes and heroines of fairy tales, we all start on our journey, our quest, sent out on it at our baptisms. We are, all of us, male and female, the younger brother, who succeeds in the quest because, unlike the elder brother, he knows he needs help; he cannot do it because he is strong and powerful. We are all, like it or not, the elder brother, arrogant and proud. We are all, male and female, the true princess who feels the pea of injustice under all those mattresses of indifference. And we all have to come to terms with the happy ending, and this may be the most difficult part of all. Never confuse fairy tale with untruth.

Alas, Lucifer, how plausible you can be, confusing us into

thinking that to speak of the Bible as myth is blasphemy. One definition of *myth* in the dictionary is *parable.* Jesus taught by telling parables. Did Jesus lie? Blaspheme?

It is Satan who is the lie, who has chosen the lie, and turned his back on truth.

A study of the myths of various religions and cultures shows us not how different we human beings are, but how alike we are in our longing for God, for the Creator who gives meaning and dignity to our lives.

I am not sure how much of the great story of Abraham, Isaac, and Jacob is literally true, how much is history, how much the overlapping of several stories. Did *both* Abraham and Isaac pretend to Abimelech that their wives were their sisters, or have the two stories mingled over the ages? Does it really matter? The mythic truths we receive from these stories enlarge our perception of the human being, and that unique being's encounters with God. When the angel of God comes to wrestle with us we must pray to be able to grapple with the unexpected truth that may be revealed to us. Because Jacob, later in the story, had the courage to ask for God's blessing, we may too.

If we take the Bible over-literally we may miss the truth of the poetry, the stories, the myths. Literalism can all too easily become judgmentalism, and Jesus warned us not to judge, that we might not be judged.

How difficult it is! When I worry about those who castigate me for not agreeing with them, am I in my turn falling into judgmentalism? It's hard not to. But not all the way, I hope. I don't want to wipe out those who disagree with me, consigning them to hell for all eternity. We are still God's children, together. At One. Even if I am angry, upset, confused, I must still see Christ and Christ's love in those whose opinions are very different from mine, or I won't find it in those whose view fits more comfortably with mine.

Dear God. What am I looking for? Help me to look for Christ.

God can use unworthy material to accomplish magnificent purposes. Worthiness is not a criterion. One can be worthy and closed, like the Pharisees in all generations and all races, all religions, failing to understand that openness to God's revelation is first and foremost. One can be worthy and so wrapped in one's worthiness that one fails to recognize the three angels who came to Abraham, or the angel Isaac knew would pick the right wife for Jacob, or those angels ascending and descending the great ladder as Jacob lay with his head on the stone. Those three great patriarchs were unworthy, but they were open to change, change in themselves, change in their understanding of their Maker. All of them saw angels. Through them we, too, can learn to be open, not closed. We, too, can have eyes and ears open to the great challenges God offers us. This does not mean fluctuation with the winds of chance or whim, but recognizing the wind of the Holy Spirit, whose sign is always the sign of love.

Jacob at last was at one with the angel. So may we be, too.

Jacob wrestled all his life—with his brother, Esau; with his father-in-law, Laban. But it was God with whom he really had to struggle.

* ✳ *

In the 1983 summer festival of children's literature at Simmons College in Boston, the overall title for the week was, "Do I Dare Disturb the Universe?" The question is asked by T.S. Eliot's J. Alfred Prufrock, and it's a question we are not usually encouraged either to ask, or to attempt to answer, particularly in our various institutions. Especially not in the church. But it's a question we need to ask, with courage, as we look at what is going on around us in the world, with wars in the name of religion accelerating all over the planet, each group claiming to represent The Truth, and occasionally proclaiming it with acts of terrorism. Universe-disturbers can be destructive as well as creative.

If we disturb the universe, no matter how lovingly, we're likely to get hurt. Nobody ever promised that universe-disturbers would have an easy time of it. Universe-disturbers make waves, rock boats, upset establishments. Gandhi upset the great British Empire. Despite his non-violence, he was unable to stop the shedding of blood, and he ended with a bullet through his heart. Anwar Sadat tried to work for peace in one of the most unpeaceful centuries in history, knowing that he might die for what he was doing, and he did.

Does it encourage our present-day universe-disturbers to know that Abraham, Isaac, and Jacob before them were universe-disturbers? Their vision of God, while undeniably masculine, was also the vision of a God who cared, who appeared to his human friends and talked with them. The patriarchs lived in a primitive, under-populated world, and yet their vision of God as Creator of all, of God who cared, of God who was part of the story, was very new.

Jesus was a great universe-disturber, so upsetting to the establishment of his day that they put him on a cross, hoping to finish him off. Those of us who try to follow his Way have a choice, either to go with him as universe-disturbers (butterflies), or to play it safe. Playing it safe ultimately leads to personal diminishment and death. If we play it safe, we resist change. Well. We all resist change, beginning as small children with our unvarying bedtime routine, continuing all through our lives. The static condition may seem like security. But if we cannot move with change, willingly or reluctantly, we are closer to death and further from life.

If we want to play it safe, we have to settle for a comfortable religion, one which will not permit questions, because questions are universe-disturbers. (Children never hesitate to ask the disturbing questions: Who was God's mother? Do numbers ever come to an end? What is the meaning of life, the universe, and everything?) If we don't allow questions, we can fool ourselves into thinking that we are capable of defining God. Every new scientific discovery about the nature of the universe has shaken one religious group or another, and yet the new discoveries do nothing whatsoever to alter the nature of the universe; they simply force us to grow in our understanding and our love of the Creator of all.

And yet, somehow or other, we've managed to keep on believing that this planet, and we who inhabit it, are the chief focus of God's concern. The idea that we may be only a small part of el's concern is very threatening.

Can God, no matter how omnipotent, keep track of it all? There are quadrillions and quintillions of galaxies, with their uncountable solar systems. The world of the microcosm is as vast as that of the macrocosm. If we did nothing all our lives but count, we could come nowhere near to counting the galaxies, much less the stars. And as for the subatomic particles . . . Can God possibly keep track of all galaxies and quarks and tachyons?

Yet in a small way even we human beings are capable of considerable multi-tracking, as Jean Houston calls it. It is said that Caesar could dictate seven letters simultaneously. During the tenure of one minister who irritated me profoundly, I found that I could listen most attentively to his sermons if, at the same time, I was memorizing the Psalms, thinking about the anthem, planning the meals, and sometimes thinking a poem. In a house full of children I was multi-tracking as my ears were open for each one of them, while I might be playing the piano, listening for the kettle to boil, and the timer to ring for the casserole in the oven. We all multi-track, even when we aren't aware of it. We've taught our computers to multi-track enormous quantities of information for us. Isn't God's ability to multi-track far greater than that of the most complex computer? God, showing Jacob the stars, needed no computer to call them all by name.

Somehow or other I must try to comprehend a God who not only can keep track of it all, but who is focused on all of it, who cares, who is aware, who is *there* for me when I call out for help, or cry a "Thank you!"

It doesn't work if I think of God as Out There. We've long known that God is not Out There, but we revert, and have to remind ourselves. I strain painfully to accept the obvious, because sometimes the obvious is not a gnat, but the whole universe.

Back when it was still possible to believe that this planet was the center of everything, that the sun and the moon and the stars were hung in the sky entirely for our benefit, it was quite possible to think of God as our Maker, Out There. God took nothing, and created a planet with water and land and fish and land animals, and proclaimed it good, looking at it all from a heavenly distance. We have too often thought of God as being *outside* the universe, creating us, and looking at what happens to us, concerned, but Out There. But as I contemplate the vastness of the night sky on a clear, cold night, God Out There does not work. Out There is *too* far out; God becomes too remote; I cannot hide under the shelter of el's protecting wings.

Scripturally, God is always in and part of Creation, walking and talking with Adam and Eve, taking Abraham out to see the stars, wrestling with Jacob.

And, in the most glorious possible demonstration of God *in* and *part of* Creation, God came to us in Jesus of Nazareth, fully participating in our human birth and life and death and offering us the glory of Easter.

If we shed our idea of God as being someone Out There, separate from all that has been made, and begin instead to think of God as within all Creation, every galaxy, every quantum, every human being, then we cannot hold ourselves "out there" either. We cannot set ourselves apart from anything that happens. Anywhere.

That's one reason some people shun fiction. Fiction draws us into participating in other lives, other countries, other ways of life or thinking. It is a way of helping us to be *in* and not *out* there.

To accept ourselves as part of everything is a big responsibility, and many would rather not face it. It is far too easy to take refuge in our own little group, rather than allowing the Creator to change us, as he changed Abraham and Isaac and Jacob.

If God created everything, if the Word called all things into being, all people are part of God's loving concern. The incarnation was not only for the Jews. Or the Christians. Christ did not come to save Christians, but to save sinners.

It's seductively pleasant to think that God loves Christians better than Buddhists or Hindhus; that, as one well-known evangelical preacher pronounced, God does not listen to the prayers of Jews. No? What about the beloved Twenty-Third Psalm? A psalm written by and for Jews, remember, with its glorious affirmation of faith: though I walk through the valley of the shadow of death, you (God) will be with me.

But what about bad prayers, ugly prayers? Damn my enemies, so that the dogs' tongues may be red with their blood. What about the Iranian terrorists? Does God hear their prayers? Or the Irish Republican Army after it has bombed a store full of Christmas shoppers? Or the Christians who feel they can't be happy in heaven unless they're watching the tortures of the damned in hell? Does God hear these prayers? I am certain that el does, even as my own worst prayers are heard. But the answer to prayer is always the answer of love, and when we are hard of heart, our ears are closed to love.

Just as a human parent listens to the demands of the children, not excluding anyone, but trying to turn anger to love, greediness to generosity, willful disobedience to responsibility, so, I believe, God does with us, and it is the Holy Spirit, praying through us, who can turn our ugliest prayers toward forgiveness and reconciliation.

How do we pray for those whose hateful actions fill us with

horror? How do we pray for the Russians who shot down a domestic plane full of unsuspecting people? for hijackers? for the Muslims who bombed our Marines in suicide missions? How do we pray for those in our own government who, I am told, did some experimenting with germ warfare in the New York subway system? or those who refuse to put anti-pollutant devices into their factories (because it is expensive enough to cut into their profits) and, wittingly, unnecessarily foul the air that even they have to breathe? Have we prayed enough? Not for revenge, but for the love that heals?

How do I keep from the pride of being judgmental? How do I open my heart in prayer? in love? The fact that I don't do it very well doesn't mean that I don't have to try. And then God can take my most fumbling, faltering prayers and make something lovely of them.

Jacob had to learn that prayer is not bargaining with God. He had to learn that the God he finally decided to accept as his own was not a God who could be tamed. When Jacob cried out for God's blessing, it was a cry to a great and extraordinary power.

Jacob learned, too, that he had to make peace with Esau, and to do so he had to be willing to open himself to change. We, too, must open ourselves to change. It is only through prayer, be it no more than a cry of "Help!" that we are given the courage to let ourselves be changed, along with all the changes in the world around us, over which we have no control.

Like Jacob, we stand once again at the threshold of great change, not only the rapidly accelerating technological changes, but change in our understanding of God's revelation of the Divine Plan, as we are challenged to grow spiritually. Why has our spiritual development lagged so agonizingly far behind our intellectual development? We have accepted most of the outward changes—electricity, the telephone, the automobile, the plane, and the computer. But spiritually we are far behind. We know

more with our minds than we do with our hearts, and this is
breaking us.

Adam and Eve, eating of the fruit of the tree of the knowledge of good and evil, precipitated themselves into a masculine
world, for knowledge, intellectual knowledge, is masculine. Wisdom, which we desperately need, is feminine, *sophia,* in Greek.
Better yet, *hagia sophia,* holy wisdom. We need holy wisdom
to help balance our misuse of the fruits of the intellect.

We must not be afraid of becoming once again in tune with
our whole selves, even when becoming whole disturbs the universe. We become whole never by being rigid or unloving or
isolating ourselves from the rest of our fellow beings, but by
opening ourselves to God's revelation of the unity of the universe.

What is our part in keeping this planet alive? Working toward
stopping the folly and horror of atomic devastation? To say that
nuclear warfare is inevitable is defeatism, not realism. As long
as there is anybody to care, to pray, to turn to God, to be willing
to be el's messenger even in unexpected ways, there is still hope.

How can we have a wide view of the unity of the universe
and of God without lapsing into a vague pantheism? If God
created *all* of Creation, if God is the author of Buddhists and
Hindhus and Jains as well as those who have "accepted Jesus
Christ as Lord," how can we avoid a wishy-washy permissiveness?

Not by retreating back into a closed system. Not by saying:
Only those who believe exactly as I do can be saved. Not by
insisting that only those whose god fits into the same box as my
god will go to heaven. Not by returning to polytheism and
proclaiming that our god is greater than the gods of other
cultures.

Paradoxically, it comes back to us, to our acceptance of
ourselves as created by God, and loved by God, no matter how
far we have fallen from God's image in us. It is not a self-satisfied,
self-indulgent acceptance, but a humble, holy, and wondrous
one.

Look! Here I am, caught up in this fragment of chronology, in this bit of bone and flesh and water which makes up my mortal body, and yet I am also part of that which is not imprisoned in time or mortality. Partaker simultaneously of the finite and the infinite, I do not find the infinite by repudiating my finiteness, but by being fully in it, in this *me* who is more than I know. This *me*, like all of creation, lives in a glorious dance of communion with all the universe. In isolation we die; in interdependence we live.

If I affirm that the God of love does indeed love all of Creation, that the salvation of the entire universe is being worked out, what does that do to my own faith?

Two young women who run a Christian bookstore in the Midwest wrote me that they were concerned as to whether or not I accept Christ as my personal Saviour. Even when I assured them that I do, they were not at all convinced that I was one of them. And perhaps the Christ I accept, by the grace of the Holy Spirit, is different from the Christ they want me to accept. But God made us all in our glorious complexity and differences; we are not meant to come off the assembly line alike, each Christian a plastic copy of every other Christian.

This insistence on sameness engenders divisions within the body of Christ, battering it still further. I have a friend who is a fine writer, openly a Christian writer, who teaches at a Christian college with a fine academic reputation. This friend has for many years been attracted to the Roman Catholic Church. I had heard new rumours about his imminent conversion, and a mutual friend of ours said to him, "Madeleine tells me that you are about to commit an absurdity."

And now that he has finally done what he considers to be going "all the way" as a Christian—he has become a Roman Catholic—I am not happy about his decision because it seems to me to emphasize the sad fact of a divided Christendom. I wish that his colleagues, instead of accepting his resignation, had gathered around him in love. I may feel that he has "committed an absurdity." But to say who is more and who is less Christian is not my privilege. No one comes to accept Christ because of personal virtue or impeccable morals, or even conviction. "No one comes to me except through the power of the Holy Spirit."

I accept Christ as my personal Saviour only because of this loving, unmerited gift of the Spirit. Christ within me and within all of Creation is what makes the stars shine at night and the sun rise in the morning. Christ was in the birth of my children and grandchildren, is in the eyes of my friends, in the blooming of the daffodils in the spring and the turning of the leaves in the autumn.

In my heart I understand the Christ given me by the love of the Spirit.

But it is not up to me to tell the Spirit where this love is going to blow. When Nicodemus came to visit Jesus at night, Jesus made it very clear to him that "the wind blows where it wishes, and you hear the sound of it, but you cannot tell from where it comes or where it goes; so is every one who is born of the Spirit."

Through the power and love of this Spirit I accept Jesus as my Saviour, the light of my life, and the light of the world. That is my affirmation and my joy.

In an interview in *Christianity Today* I was asked, "Are you a universalist?"

My reply is as true now as it was then. "No. I am not a universalist. I am a particular incarnationalist. I believe that we can understand cosmic questions only through particulars. I can understand God only through one specific particular, the Incarnation of Jesus of Nazareth. This is the ultimate particular, which gives me my understanding of the Creator and of the beauty of life. I believe that God loved us so much that he came to us as a human being to show us his love."

We live in an open, interacting, creative universe, and to try to close it into a safe little system is a danger to ourselves and a danger to everyone we touch. But if we are willing to be a small part of a great whole, then we know that no part in the dance is too small, too unimportant to make a difference. We are all like the butterfly in the amazing, unexpected magnitude of our effect. Even when we feel most helpless, when events we cannot control or prevent pile up, even in our most bitter brokenness, we do have our role in the working out of the great plan.

May God, through the Christ shown us by the Holy Spirit, open our hearts in love.

Alleluia.

Angel
Unaware

6

THE WEDNESDAY OF THANKSGIVING WEEKEND, 1983, was cold in New York, and dark. But through the darkness came a sign of great hope.

One of the advantages of living largely on the crowded island of Manhattan is that people tend to come through the big city, and so I see many friends, either en route to another destination, or sometimes simply here for a few days in New York. The day before Thanksgiving, 1983, was such a day of friends, a day that made me more than thankful to be in the city.

At 12:15 on Wednesdays there is a communion service at the Cathedral of St. John. It is held in one of the small chapels behind the high altar, and that Wednesday I joyfully found myself sharing bread and wine and prayer and friendship with a diverse group, from Korea, Minnesota, Illinois. After the Eucharist six of us went across the street to our favourite Hungarian restaurant for lunch.

On the Sunday evening before, all of us, in our various parts of the world, had watched the television movie, *The Day After,* about the horror of a nuclear war. In his homily the minister who had celebrated the eucharist had talked about the Christian response to the possibilities and impossibilities the movie depicted.

Actually I had (as it were) seen the same movie thirty years earlier, in the fifties, in black and white TV. It took place in a suburb of New York, rather than Kansas, but the general story line was the same: the dropping of bombs on the city with total death and destruction, and then the horrors awaiting those in the suburbs who had survived—radiation sickness, starvation, looting, and the shooting of and by those trying to defend their homes and their dwindling food supplies. Desperate, untenable awfulness. In his homily the minister had talked of the severe serenity with which the believer should meet anything, even this, and of God's great and terrible gift of free will. How much does God interfere with our misuse of free will, we wondered? In that day's mail I had received a letter with the question, "Is God going to allow us to blow ourselves up?"

Among the six of us was Mel Lorentzen, a teacher and writer from Wheaton. He told us a true story about his friend, the opera singer Jerome Hines. In 1961, Hines was in Russia, singing Mussorgsky's great opera, *Boris Godounov.* Hugh and I saw a superb production of this opera in the Kirov theatre when we were in Leningrad. It was an opera I had always wanted to see, partly because of my mother's recounting of the first time she and father had heard it. When the great bells for the coronation music started, she said, they had stood up to see the orchestra, and the sound of bells was coming from two grand pianos, and their spines tingled. When Hugh and I stopped at Intourist in Leningrad and saw that *Boris* was playing that night, I let out an adolescent shriek of enthusiasm (something that evidently doesn't often happen in Intourist offices) and we were given the Royal Box—yes, it's still there! Although we shared it with several others.

So *Boris* has a special place in my heart.

Jerome Hines, who had learned the role in Russian, was to be the first non-Russian to sing the great opera in the original tongue.

At the close of the opera Boris has lost his crown and his throne, and the traditional ending is for Boris to roll from his throne in an anguish of defeat. Jerome Hines felt that Mussorgsky's music did not justify this interpretation, that the music is triumphant and therefore Boris's yielding of his power is part of that triumph, and he played it that way. The final performance in Moscow was to be televised, but at the last minute the singers were told that there would be no television cameras because Khrushchev was going to be in the audience.

Jerome Hines is a man of prayer, and while he was in Russia, prayer for Khrushchev had been foremost in his mind, not deliberately, but because the name *Khrushchev* kept being "given" to him. He sang superbly that night, and at the close of the opera, instead of the usual humiliating tumbling from the throne in defeat, he took off his crown and flung his arms heavenwards in triumph. The audience went wild with applause and cheers.

Khrushchev came backstage with an interpreter, to say how much he had enjoyed the performance, and as he was leaving, Hines said, in Russian, "God bless you, sir." Khrushchev turned, looked him in the eye without answering, and left.

There is a mighty time difference between Moscow and Washington. It couldn't have been too long after Khrushchev returned from the opera that night that President John F. Kennedy called Moscow. This was the time of the Cuban missile crisis, and Kennedy gave Khrushchev an ultimatum—Get out of Cuba.

And the Russians withdrew.

What might have happened if Khrushchev had not gone to see *Boris Godounov*? if Hines had not turned Boris's defeat into a triumph? if Hines had not said, from his heart, to the atheist head of an atheist country, "God bless you, sir"?

God, without interfering in human free will, was part of the story. The pattern was worked out through the music, through the singer, through the head of state, but without coercion. The opportunity was given, but it was not mandated.

This is for me a perfect example of how God calls us to write the story *with him,* lovingly, creatively, of our own free will.

God does not want us to blow ourselves up. He will not stop us if we insist on self-destruction, but every possible creative alternative will be offered us, and the Hines-Khrushchev story is only one example of disaster averted by love and prayer. It gives me great hope.

God sends angels in unexpected and mysterious ways. We children of the Highest are asked to be angels—messengers—whether we are aware of our role or not. We are called on to be angels not by God Out There, but by God In Here, *with us,* Emmanuel. May God continue to send angels. May we continue to hear, as Jerome Hines heard. And as Khrushchev, the God-denyer, surely heard.

Was Jacob, wrestling with the angel, a stranger person to be grappled with by God then Khrushchev?

Jerome Hines was a universe-disturber, a creative universe-disturber. Hines could have played the role of Boris the traditional way, safely. He could have refused the arduous task of learning the opera in Russian. He could have shunned the risk of calling for God's blessing on a man whom he knew denied God. He could have declined to pray for Khrushchev. But he took the risk.

If we refuse to take the risk of being vulnerable we are already half dead. If we are half dead we don't have to starve with the people of Ethiopia. We don't have to share the terrible living conditions of old people struggling to exist on dwindling social security payments in our overcrowded, hostile cities. We don't have to smell the stench of filth, and disease, and hunger in the favelas and barrios.

We are not all called to go to El Salvador, or Moscow, or Calcutta, or even the slums of New York, but none of us will escape the moment when we have to decide whether to withdraw, to play it safe, or to act upon what we prayerfully believe to be right, knowing that with all our prayers we may be wrong, and knowing that we will probably be punished by those who do not want universe-disturbers to stand up and be counted.

Perhaps what we are called to do may not seem like much, but the butterfly is a small creature to affect galaxies thousands of light years away.

* ✳ *

Not all universe-disturbers are creative; not all are listening to God's call. Many are destructively following the fallen angels, from Atilla the Hun, to Hitler, to Farrakan, to rapists, and terrorists.

Jerome Hines was one of God's angels. He did not go to Russia to be an angel. He went because he was an opera singer by training and vocation, and a man of prayer. God can use us wherever we are, in whatever we do. We do not have to do or be anything special in order to bring hope to the world. We may not even know when God has used one of us as an angel unaware, and that's just as well. Our part lies in being open, not to God Out There, but In Here, *with us, in us*.

When we visualize God as being only up in heaven, and heaven as being apart from earth, we lose the immediacy of God as part of the story, part of our being, as intimate as was the angel who wrestled all night with Jacob and changed his

97

story forever. God was not something apart from Creation, or apart from daily life, God was there, marvellously, terribly there.

✳ ✳ ✳

If God is in and part of all creation, then any part can be a messenger, an angel. Sometimes our very questions are angelic. Questions allow us to grow and develop and change in our understanding of ourselves and of God, so that nothing that happens, and nothing that science discovers, is frightening, or disturbs our faith in God.

Some scientists in their arrogance have done terrible things. But the great scientists are humble, and have imaginations as vivid as any poet's—"The butterfly effect," for instance. What a marvellous concept, and what a marvellous way of expressing it, and by a scientist, not an artist!

The quark, one of the smallest, if not *the* smallest, of our subatomic particles, is named from James Joyce's *Finnegans Wake*. The world of subatomic particles is so extraordinary that even to contemplate it implies an open imagination.

We have discovered the world of subatomic physics because we have split the atom. This has revealed many things which are horrible indeed. A considerable number of scientists have repented of the use made of their discoveries. True repentance opens our eyes to the God who heals and redeems.

As a nation we have yet to come to terms with our fire bombs which destroyed German cities and their civilian population during World War Two. We have yet to come to terms with having dropped not one, but two atom bombs, leaving the horror of death and radiation, maiming men, and women, and children who had nothing to do with battle lines. Part of our fascination with the atom bomb may be caused by our refusal, as a nation, to repent. We have yet to come to terms with Vietnam, and Lebanon, and El Salvador, because repentance is no longer part of our national vocabulary.

What would those who were responsible for the making of the automobile have done if some kind of prescience had shown them that the death toll from automobile accidents is already greater than the death toll of all of the world's wars put together? What would the scientists working on the splitting of the atom have done if they could have foreseen Hiroshima and Nagasaki? Many of the scientists who worked on early fusion and fission were appalled at the gigantic Pandora's box they had opened. A considerable number of those who had approached the work as humanistic atheists turned from their atheism to become deeply committed theists. A good many, not all, but a good many, looked at what they had unleashed and got down on their knees.

And the power of prayer is greater than the Pentagon. It is greater than the greed and corruption which can still conceive of a nuclear holocaust as survivable. It is greater than the bomb. It can help bring wisdom to our knowledge, wisdom which is all that will keep us from destroying ourselves with our knowledge.

In an accidental and godless universe, where the human race on this particular planet in this particular galaxy appeared by happenstance, there would be very little hope. But in a purposeful universe created by a caring, loving God, there is great hope that ultimately el's purposes will be worked out in history.

My father was gassed in the trenches of the First World War because he would not let his men go where he had not gone first, and this concerned leadership spared the others from the gas. That war, which ended shortly before I was born, was closer to the old hand-to-hand warfare than the present impersonal ways of combat. Every year on Armistice Day, as it used to be called, the phone rang and kept on ringing, with one after another of Father's men calling him to thank him, and to see how he was. These calls continued year after year, until his death. And that, to me is a sign of hope, as Jerome Hines is a sign of hope.

It is an example of community, of a community which lasted long after the physical proximity of those involved had been broken and they had scattered to many different parts of the world. But what had been the heart of that community still endured.

Quaker writer Parker Palmer says,

Most of us fear community because we think it will call us away from ourselves. We are afraid that in community our sense of self will be overpowered by the identity of the group. We pit individuality and community against one another, as if a choice had to be made, and increasingly we choose the former.

But what a curious conception of self we have! We have forgotten that the self is a moving intersection of many other selves. We are formed by the lives which intersect with ours. The larger and richer our community, the larger and richer is the content of self. There is no individuality without community.

That community of men calling my father, one after another, year after year on Armistice Day, told me a great deal about the individual person who was also my father.

The war in which my father served was followed by another war, and another, and it seems that war will never cease. We need—as a country, as individuals who cannot separate ourselves from either our country or the world—to face what we have done, and ask forgiveness. Forgiveness from God, from those we have hurt, and, what is harder, from ourselves. Then we may be able to regain a sense of wonder about our small planet and the fragile life it sustains, and once again become the good stewards God called us to be.

It is, as always, paradox. God will not force us, take away our free will, demand that we do the work of love like robots. We are free not to listen, to damn our enemies rather than pray for them. God will not intervene in our self-destruction unless we are willing. We will not hear God unless we listen. We can't just turn it all over to God; it is up to us, too. And yet, we can't do anything until we turn it all over to God. This turning it over is not a passive sitting back—an okay, you take care of it, Pop— but an active listening to the power of love, and a willingness to love our enemies as well as our friends. ("God bless you, sir," Jerome Hines said, and meant it.)

It was easier for Esau to forgive Jacob for his treachery than it was for Jacob to believe in or accept Esau's forgiveness.

When I walk my dog at night, the route on the way home takes me past a Buddhist temple with a terrace on which stands a huge statue of Saint Shinran Shunin, a Buddhist saint of the twelfth century. This particular statue was in Hiroshima when the bomb fell, and was sent by the Buddhists of that city to the Buddhists in New York as a symbol of forgiveness and hope. Each night as my dog and I walk by the great statue, the huge bulk of metal wearing a patina I have never seen on another statue, I say, "Good night, Saint Shinran. Forgive us, and help us," and for me, at that moment, Saint Shinran is one of God's angels. Am I worshipping a pagan saint? A lifeless hunk of metal? No! It is an attitude of heart, a part of turning to Christ.

I rejoiced to read in William Johnston's *The Inner Eye of Love* that Saint Shinran rebelled against legalism and proclaimed "the pre-eminence of faith and grace," and that "he has been frequently compared to Luther."

We don't have to drop nuclear bombs again. We don't have to blow ourselves up. We've had the capacity to destroy all life on this planet with germ warfare since World War One, and we haven't done it. But we need all the prayers we can possibly get, all the openness of love, no matter how much it costs. And we need to look for angels.

I wish that the made-for-television film, "The Day After," had added just a minute to its bleak and hopeless ending, that it had shown Lawrence, Kansas, in the spring, or harvest time, that it had ended with the wedding which was halted by the bombing. I wish it had ended with a message of hope: *this* is what we are working for—life, not death.

It is not good to send out only negative vibrations, to offer no alternative to disaster. We need positive energy, too, which is something we can do something about, stopping ourselves when we are feeling negative, and looking for something positive. If sound waves stay in the ether for ever, then the voices of those men who never forgot to call my father are still there, too. The words of love are strong. We need to listen to them.

We have lived with the possibility of extinction since the planet was formed, extinction by natural calamity, by the shifting of the planet on its axis, by epidemic, by our own avariciousness. It should have taught us to live more fully—savouring each moment, using each day fully, seeing each sunrise and sunset and evening star, turning our hearts to those we love—but by and large we've gone on as usual, dragged down by ordinariness. But even if we can expect to live out our full life span, nothing is ordinary. Life itself is extraordinary. *Little lamb, who made thee?* Blake asks. *Dost thou know who made thee?* He also asks: *Tyger, tyger, burning bright in the forests of the night, what immortal hand or eye framed thy fearful symmetry?*

* ✳ *

The sign of hope that Mel gave us in the story of Jerome Hines was with me as we gathered together for Thanksgiving dinner the next day, as we put on the banquet cloth, the best china and crystal and silver, lit candles, and held hands all around for grace.

Did Abraham ever gather all his various children and their mothers together for a meal of thanks and rejoicing? Did Isaac and Rebekah call Jacob and Esau to share a meal, thanking God for the fruits of the land and for Esau's mighty hunting? Did Jacob and his wives sit down with all their sons and their one daughter?

After Abraham's feast for three angels, and Lot's festive meal for two angels, it should be clear to us that there has always been a sacramental aspect to a shared meal. The guest at our table must be honoured thereafter; you cannot break bread with someone and then stab that person. But if the meal has been desacralized, that obligation no longer holds.

As a twentieth-century society we have desacralized meal-times as we have almost all aspects of our lives. At my alma mater the students still eat in the dining room of their house, at small tables, taking turns with the serving and washing up, but at most colleges and universities there is now something called Food Service, and meals are cafeteria style, catch as catch can (and usually make the institutional food I griped about seem marvellously gourmet food by comparison!).

Even at home families do not always eat together, because of conflicts in schedule, so the meal is further desacralized with plates in laps before the TV, and loses its link with the heavenly banquet.

How do we regain the meal as sacrament? as a foretaste of the at-one-ness to come? Does something as simple as a family meal make that much difference?

It does, oh, it does.

If there is a sense of sacrament about the meal, then it can spread out to all areas of life. No one with a vital sense of the sacred could go into a church or synagogue and commit acts of vandalism. And it took an overwhelming sense of the sacred for Jerome Hines to be an angel unaware when he sang *Boris* in Moscow.

Jerome Hines was granted the knowledge of the creative result of his prayer for Khrushchev, and he is a man so committed to God that he can accept the understanding without falling into pride, into taking personal credit for what he did. It is probably a blessing that most of us are not granted this knowledge. We do like to be patted on the back, to be told that what we did was terrific, or significant. And it sometimes is. But we never act alone. We simply participate in God's action. It may be action which is expressed through us, but the love is always God's, and it is our joy to be allowed to share.

The butterfly does not understand that the beating of its wings can be felt in distant galaxies. The butterfly is simply, fully, and beautifully a butterfly.

So let us try to be simply, fully, and beautifully human beings, bearing within us the image of God.

Bless
the
Bastard

7

JEROME HINES PRAYED FOR the atheist leader of an atheist country, and whether the atheists like it or not, theirs is a powerful religion. We, too, are called to pray for those whose religion differs from ours, those who condone acts of terrorism, who are zealots espousing destructive causes. We are also called to pray for those whose god is different from ours, and yet who live quiet, godly lives. How do we pray? Simply by offering to God our concern for all of Creation, not coercively or manipulatively, but lovingly, for it all belongs to the Creator. We separate ourselves from the stars and from God when we separate ourselves from any part of Creation.

But a wariness of "the others" seems always to have been part of human nature. The patriarchs were uneasy with peoples of other tribes and other gods, as we may be uneasy with Muslims and Parsees and Quiztanos. But today, with all the instant information from TV and radio, newspapers and magazines, we have less excuse for our lack of understanding.

As Abraham had not wanted Isaac to marry a foreigner, so Rebekah and Isaac did not want their sons (particularly Jacob) to marry any of the women from Heth, who worshipped different gods, who were "them," not "us," and so Isaac charged Jacob not to take a wife of the daughters of Canaan.

> And God Almighty bless you, and make you fruitful, and multiply you, and give you the blessing of Abraham, that you may inherit the land where you are a stranger, the land which God gave to Abraham.

Paternalistic, nationalistic, and in terms of the late twentieth-century, distressing.

But Abraham and Sarah, Isaac and Rebekah, Jacob and Rachel, did not live in the late twentieth-century, and we abuse all that we have learned in the intervening centuries if we try to rewrite history. Yet that is what we are unwittingly doing as we attempt to change language into what is called inclusive language, which ends up being more sexist than the language it is trying to replace.

Even by continuing to link Sarah with Abraham, Rebekah with Isaac, Rachel with Jacob, I'm slightly changing the emphasis, and I'd better be aware what I'm doing.

Abraham, Isaac, and Jacob were forefathers. Sarah and Rebekah and Rachel were interesting women, but they are seldom referred to as foremothers, though that is what they were. Sarah, Rebekah, and Rachel lived in a world of patriarchs, not matriarchs, and it is futile to try to see their culture as something it was not. We may hope to influence present and future history, but we must beware of altering the past unless we really and truly know what we are doing and have been called by an angel to do so.

T. S. Eliot (in *Selected Prose*) says that it is not "preposterous that the past should be altered by the present, as much as the present is directed by the past. And the poet who is aware of this will be aware of great difficulties and responsibilities."

Such a poet is needed now; a casual or irresponsible altering of the past can be very dangerous.

The tents of Abraham, Isaac, and Jacob were not far from the tribes who worshipped the goddesses, the matriarchal religions which so upset the patriarchal Hebrew. But Jacob and Rachel did not live with Astarte, or Ashtaroth, or Ishtar, or any of the female goddesses, and there is no point in pretending that their world understood that the feminine is as important as the masculine. I suspect that our forefathers were afraid of the feminine, in the world, in themselves. That fear is still very much alive today, fear of the nurturing darkness of the womb, of the intuitive self which can give insights unavailable to the conscious will, of the tenderness of love with all its vulnerability. And that fear makes the feminine in Jacob all the more remarkable.

Our religion needs to change as our knowledge and understanding grow, but beware if we change it thoughtlessly. The new translations of the creed are a case in point. I love the new Episcopal prayer book, love it enough to feel free to criticize it where I feel it has fallen short of its best. We used to say that Jesus was *conceived by the Holy Spirit.* Now we say *He was conceived by the power of the Holy Spirit.* That's not the same thing at all. We are all (or should be) conceived by the power of the Holy Spirit. To say that Jesus was conceived *by* the Holy Spirit is far more exciting. The angel came to Mary and told her that "The Holy Ghost shall come upon you."

It's a shocking myth, but it's been our myth for a long time; we've held to it for two thousand years, even though it has kept some people from being Christian because they "cannot cope with the virgin birth." The virgin birth has never been a major stumbling block in my struggle with Christianity; it's far less mind-boggling than the Power of all Creation stooping so low as to become one of us. But I find myself disturbed at the changing, by some committee or other, of the myth which brought God and the human creature together in marvellous at-one-ment, as Jacob's ladder brought heaven and earth together. That's the wonder, that God can reach out and become one with that which has been created. This at-one-ment should not be broken thoughtlessly. Nor should we fall into that trap of rigid literalism. We don't have to know the *how* of parthogenesis. And even the word parthogenesis is a stumbling block, trying to use scientific jargon to express what is inexpressible mystery. All we need to know is God's terrible closeness, an intimacy which hallows our createdness.

A minister friend said, "It's very nice to know we're related to God on his mother's side."

The great mysteries of the creed are an affirmation which I find difficult to make in the new language which is watered down to make it easier, and which offends me because it tries to put the radically unbelievable glory by which I live into rational, palatable language, which I find so unpalatable that I gag on it. Not that I am against contemporary translations; I am strongly for them. But I want them to be in the very best "language of the people," not impoverished by unimaginative realism.

When our children were very young we started reading the King James translation of the Bible to them, and they weren't old enough for it, and were bored. So we switched to J.B. Phillips' translation. One day our little boy was sent from the table for some misdemeanor and told to stay away for five minutes. At the end of five minutes he came rushing down the stairs crying, "What did I miss?" J. B. Phillips' translation worked beautifully for him. And Phillips still works for me, too, far better than some of the more recent translations which are tinged with condescension toward both the human creature and the Creator.

But don't let's stop trying. We need to do better in our new translations than we are presently doing. In trying to use inclusive language, we have blundered into inconclusive language.

What's wrong? Our language does indeed need changing as we come to accept the feminine as well as the masculine, the intuitive as well as the intellectual. But thus far our attempts are not working. I suspect that this is because the inadequacy of our language is a symptom of something far deeper, a brokenness between the human being and the Maker, and an equal brokenness within ourselves. We have lost the ability to see the marvellous ladder of angels uniting heaven and earth, and so we have become earth-bound, separated from the stars and the music of the spheres.

Our lacks in language are a reflection of our brokenness. When we spend our energy futilely trying to fix pronouns, we can forget that we may be bleeding to death.

If we could stop focussing on symptoms, and allow God to heal us with creative love, the healing of language would follow.

Man, the image of God, male and female. Whole. Our own image of God is unavoidably anthropomorphic. As human beings, we think in human terms; there is, for us, no other way. But the image of God within us is love. And God is a spirit.

We are reminded in the New Testament that we are the temple of the Holy Spirit. We honour our bodies because they are made to contain the Holy Spirit, the image of God, but they are not themselves what they contain. I have sometimes been most awesomely aware of the image of God in someone whose body is distorted; I saw the image in an old woman so crippled with arthritis that her body was nothing but knots; I saw the image in a young man born with terrible deformities; the image is there for us in the suffering servant of Isaiah, "his appearance was so marred, beyond human semblance . . . he had no form or comeliness that we should look at him, and no beauty that we should desire him. He was despised and rejected by men, a man of sorrows, and acquainted with grief; and as one from whom men hide their faces he was despised, and we esteemed him not."

If we bear the image of love in our own flawed, human bodies, it is this love which will ultimately renew language. And then perhaps we will be given a truly great writer, like Chaucer, or Shakespeare, to transform language with genius.

Religion and language are like rivers, constantly flowing from the same source, as we respond to all that is happening in the world around us. Maybe one day we'll get the hang of it, the yin and the yang of it. Language changes most graciously through poets and storytellers, and most clumsily when it is being manipulated by reformers and committees.

I saw a small sign in one of the offices of Bethel Seminary in Minnesota. *God so loved the world that he did not send a committee.*

Not a committee, but the Word of love.

✳ ✳ ✳

In Berdyaev's *Revelation and Truth,* which I continued to read during jury duty, he wrote that the age of the Old Testament was the Age of the Father. The New Testament was the Age of the Son. And he referred to the time at which he was writing— several decades ago—as the Age of the Spirit.

We are now groping slowly toward the Age of the Trinity, of wholeness. The fact that we Christians are beginning to recognize our brokenness, our fragmentation, is a sign of this healing movement. We speak now of holistic medicine. We speak of certain people as being holy, which really means being whole. We are turning once again to the insights of myth, the lessons of story, as we seek to move beyond the limits of the intellect.

The Holy Trinity contains knowledge and wisdom and male and female and child and sage and artist and holy fool and philosopher and mathematician and musician and a few million other qualities. The glory of the stars at night is an image of wholeness, for the universe is a unity. The smallest subatomic particles have their share in this unity, in the perfecting of the pattern.

The human family, too, is an icon of the Trinity, but how we have defaced and cracked the icon. The sacredness of family is desacralized by the breakdown of family life and the so-called sexual revolution which promised freedom, but which has brought about alienation and terrible loneliness. When we focus on one aspect of the Trinity, or of ourselves, at the expense of the whole, we blunder into disaster.

Maybe it was time for the sexual revolution, but it, like all revolutions, went further than the initial vision. Abortion is an ugly and unsolved problem, and while the theological answer may be clear, easy answers produce such unloving actions as the throwing of bombs. Herpes and AIDS have become epidemic, terrifying as the Black Plague. We may be more open about sex, but we have emphasized the purely physical at the expense of the fullness of love.

At first Jacob loved Rachel because she was beautiful. But then the love strengthened as they came to know each other in the truest, deepest ways.

No matter how objective I try to be when I read the story of Jacob, or any part of Scripture, I am reading into it, willy nilly, my own prejudices, hopes, culture. This is inevitable. I see past history from my place within present history. It is impossible to see it exactly as it was for even the most objective of historians. It is easiest to understand when it is in the form of story. Even so, I still read into it my own questions. My understanding of Isaac and Rebekah, Jacob and Rachel, is formed by my understanding of all my encounters with people. Did Rebekah love her son, Jacob, more than she loved her husband, Isaac? She was willing to deceive Isaac in order to get the blessing for the younger, favoured son, Jacob. It was Rebekah, his mother, who told Jacob what to do, who was the initiator of the plot to deceive blind old Isaac. And she deceived her son, Esau, too, the hairy one, who was loved of his father.

Isaac was old, and nearly blind, and he called Esau, his eldest son, and Esau said, "Behold, here am I."

And Isaac said, "Behold, now I am old, and I know not the day of my death. Therefore, I pray you, take your quiver and bow, and go out into the field, and take me some venison, and make me some savoury meat, such as I love, and bring it to me, that I may eat, and that my soul may bless you before I die."

Rebekah heard this, so she went to Jacob and told him, and said, "Do what I command you. Go to the flock and fetch me two good kids of the goats, and I will make them savoury meat for your father, such as he loves, and you shall bring it to your father, that he may eat it, and bless you before his death."

And Jacob said to Rebekah his mother, "But Esau my brother is a hairy man, and I am a smooth man. Perhaps my father will feel me, and know that I am deceiving him, and will give me a curse instead of a blessing."

And his mother said, "Upon me be the curse, my son. Just obey me and go fetch the kids."

So Jacob obeyed his mother, and she made savoury meat, such as Isaac loved. And she took Esau's best clothes, and put them on Jacob. And she put the skins of the kids and goats upon his hands, and upon the smooth of his neck. And she gave the savoury meat and the bread, which she had prepared, to Jacob.

And Jacob went to his father, and said, "My father," and

Isaac said, "Here I am. Who are you?"

And Jacob said to his father, "I am Esau, your first born. I have done what you asked of me. So sit and eat my venison, that your soul may bless me."

Was old Isaac a little suspicious? He asked a penetrating question—how had his son found the venison so quickly?

And Jacob answered, "Because the Lord, your God, brought it to me."

The Lord, your God? Was God not yet Jacob's God? Did he have to wait for the night of wrestling with the angel to know God? Isaac, still seeming suspicious, told his son to come closer to him, to be felt.

And Jacob went near his father, and Isaac felt him, and said, "The voice is Jacob's voice, but the hands are the hands of Esau."

And Isaac did not recognize Jacob because his hands were hairy, so he blessed him, and he asked, "Are you truly my son, Esau?"

And Jacob said, "I am."

And Isaac ate of the savoury venison, and drank some wine, and then he said, "Come near me, and kiss me, my son."

And Jacob came near and kissed him, and Isaac smelled the smell of his clothes, and blessed him, and said, "See, the smell of my son is like the smell of a field which the Lord has blessed. May God give you dew from heaven and the richness of the earth, and plenty of corn and wine. Let people serve you, and nations bow down to you. Be lord over your brother. Let the sons of your mother bow down to you. Cursed be everyone who curses you, and blessed be everyone who blesses you."

And so Isaac gave to Jacob the blessing which should have gone to Esau.

> And it came to pass as soon as Isaac had finished blessing Jacob, and Jacob had scarcely left the presence of Isaac, that Esau came in from hunting. And he also had made savoury meat and brought it to his father, saying, "Let my father arise and eat of his son's venison, that your soul may bless me."
>
> And Isaac his father said to him, "Who are you?"
>
> And he said, "I am your son, your first born, Esau."
>
> And Isaac trembled greatly and said, "Who? Where is he who took venison and brought it to me? I ate all of it before you came, and I blessed him. Yes, and he shall be blessed."

For a blessing, once given, cannot be retracted.

> And when Esau heard the words of his father, he gave a great and bitter cry, and said to his father, "Bless me, even me also, O my father." And he wept.

But Isaac had given the blessing reserved for the first son. It had been given, and he could not take it back. He said,

> "Far from the richness of the earth shall be your dwelling place, far from the dew that falls from heaven. You shall live by your sword, and you shall serve your brother. But when you win your freedom, you shall shake his yoke from your neck."

Esau's story is a tragic one, and all the more so because of his unloveliness, covered with red hair, smelling of the blood of the animals he had killed, over-easily duped by his brother. (And by his mother, though he may not have known that.) One can hardly blame him for deciding that after Isaac had died, and the mourning period was over, he would kill his brother.

He may have shouted this aloud in his outrage, for someone told Rebekah, and she called Jacob and urged him to leave quickly and go to her brother, Laban, in Haran, and stay there until Esau's anger had cooled.

So Jacob left, taking with him Isaac's blessing.

＊ ✳ ＊

We take both blessing and cursing much too casually nowadays. When someone sneezes we say, "Bless you," hardly thinking. It used to be believed that when one sneezes one is very close to death, and therefore to say, "Bless you," truly meant something important. It does. We need to reawaken our sense of blessing.

Often I hear a casual "dammit," meaning nothing but momentary annoyance, but to damn someone is serious indeed, because even our casual irritations leave their imprint and cannot be erased.

How do we learn to bless, rather than damn, those with whom we disagree, those whom we fear, those who are different?

Cursing is more a matter of intent than of language. Listen to a group of construction workers, or stage hands, and you will hear the four-letter words fly, but more likely they are used with affection, rather than malice. The liberal use of such words is often no more than regional or vocational vocabulary.

Whereas someone can say, calmly, "I do want you to know that I understand why you did this, and that I forgive you," and more venom can drip from those words than from any amount of casual profanity. Most Christians object to swearing because it is specifically forbidden by Christ in the fifth chapter of Matthew's gospel. There is, of course, a difference between using God's name "in vain" and merely vulgar, gutter words.

But what offended Jesus was hardness of heart, not laxness of language, which often stems from paucity of vocabulary. I suspect that if we could have heard the speech of some of Jesus' followers we might be disturbed. It was those whose lives were whitewashed on the outside, but full of dead bones inside, who made Jesus angry.

Certainly I am not advocating coarse or careless language. Far from it. But I am concerned about the intent behind the words which may be more significant than the words themselves. When I read a novel I am concentrating on the characters' hearts, and if the heart is warm, and open to growth in love, I probably won't even notice a few racy words. After all, I've worked in the theatre and heard the stage hands. I spend much of the year living on Manhattan's upper west side. I've learned that it is what's behind the words that truly counts.

Not long ago in Toronto, I was on a radio program with two Canadian writers. I was given some of their books to read, and was told that one of them, Kevin Major, "uses questionable language." That night I read his *Hold Fast,* a novel set in Newfoundland. I thought that it was a fine book, and that the language, according to the situation and place, was not at all inappropriate. And on page seven, Major himself expressed exactly what I feel. His protagonist says of his uncle, "The swear words, when he spitted them out of him, was almost enough to curl up my guts. Not the words, that was nothing. I was use to that. But the way he said them. People swears in different ways. Dad use to swear and he hardly had a clue he was swearing it. But the way the same words came out of Uncle Ted, it was like a set of teeth, tearing into her."

Those of us blessed with a good education have the responsibility to use vocabulary judiciously, not carelessly. And to bless, not curse. To affirm, not damn.

In this muddled world it is not always easy to bless, but that is our calling. To curse is not only to wound another, it is to put ourselves in bondage. To bless is to be made free to bear God's love.

* ✳ *

A writer I admire horrified me by saying that perhaps we will see Jesus coming again on a mushroom cloud, that the sign of the Second Coming will be the roiling cloud of an exploded nuclear bomb. No! Everything in me rejects the conjunction of an act of destructive hate with God's act of Creative love. And yet I have come to realize with sadness mingled with horror that some Christians are beginning to equate the Second Coming with nuclear disaster.

That cannot be. Of one thing only am I certain: the Second Coming is an action of Love. The judgment of God is the judgment of love, not of power plays or vindication or hate. The Second Coming is the redemption of the entire cosmos, not just one small planet.

St. Paul, writing to the people of Rome, reminds us that "The creation waits with eager longing for the revealing of the sons of God . . . the creation itself will be set free from its bondage of decay and obtain the glorious liberty of the children of God."

All of Creation groans in travail. All will be redeemed in God's fullness of time, all, not just the small portion of the population who have been given the grace to know and accept Christ. All the strayed and stolen sheep. All the little lost ones.

To equate the Second Coming with nuclear holocaust is to expect God to curse Creation, not to bless; to look for hell, not heaven, which is a kind of blasphemy, for we are called to live in hope. A Second Coming on a sulphurous, radioactive death-dealing cloud would be a victory for Satan, not Christ.

It would seem that the majority of those who see nuclear

warfare and the Second Coming together are those who see Christ's coming in glory as exclusively for them and their fellow brand of believers. They, and they only, will be raptured up to heaven, and everybody else will burn in hell. Heaven is somewhat like a restricted country club for a favoured few, and the Lord of Love is quite willing to curse everybody else.

The Lord of Love?

There's a story of a good man who dies and goes to heaven, and who is welcomed at the pearly gates, which are thrown open for him to enter. He goes through them in a daze of bliss, because it is everything he has been taught, golden streets, milk and alabaster and honey and golden harps. He wanders the streets lost in happiness, until after a while he realizes that he is all alone; he hasn't seen anybody at all. He walks and walks, and he sees nobody.

So he goes back to the gates, and asks, "Peter?"

"Yes, my son?"

"This really is heaven?"

"Oh, yes, my son. Don't you like it?"

"Oh, it's just wonderful! But where is everybody? Where are the prophets? Where is the Holy Family? Where are the saints?"

Peter looks at him kindly. "Oh, them? They're all down in hell, ministering to the damned. If you'd like to join them, I'll show you the way."

* * *

Jesus said, "And many false prophets shall rise, and shall deceive many. And because iniquity shall abound, the love of many shall wax cold."

The prophets who are discovering and pointing out devil-worshippers, who sniff out pornography and dirty words, are also among those who equate the Second Coming with Judgment Day.

Cold. It is coldness of heart that prophesies falsely.

Jesus continues, "For there shall arise false Christs, and false prophets, who shall show great signs and wonders, so that, if it were possible, they shall deceive the very elect. But of the day and hour no one knows, no, not the angels of heaven, but my father only."

Throughout the centuries there have been countless false prophets proclaiming the end of the world. As the first millennium approached, a great many Christians thought that with the year One Thousand would come Judgment Day. Since then there have been many other predictions of the world's end, including a goodly number in our own century. Some of the prophets have backed their predictions with quotations from John's Revelation, but that great visionary book is not to be taken literally. It is a sign of pride to think we can predict the end which Jesus said was hidden even from the angels. We do not know when it is coming. We must prepare, lest the bridegroom's coming catch us unaware. But we do not know. Being prepared, and knowing when the bridegroom is coming are two very different things. Jesus was emphatic about that.

How do we tell the false prophet from the true prophet? The true prophet seldom predicts the future. The true prophet warns us of our present hardness of heart, our prideful presuming to know God's mind. And the final test of the true prophet is love. God came to us as Jesus because of love. All the ills of the Fall will be righted and redeemed in the Second Coming because of love.

We must be careful in our right and proper protests against the folly of nuclear stockpiling that we are protesting truly, that we are not being false prophets fearing only for our own selves, our own families, our own country. Our concern must be for everybody, for the Russians, the Chinese, the Iranians, for our entire fragile planet, and everybody on it. And for all of God's creation, because we cannot blow ourselves up in isolation.

Indeed, we must protest with loving concern for the entire universe.

The Old Testament prophets were often reluctant. The false prophets took pride in their prophesying and told the people what they wanted to hear, and so were popular. Whereas the true prophets, warning the people of the consequences of their evil actions, were anything but popular. They risked their lives. A mark of the true prophet in any age is humility, self-emptying so there is room for God's Word. The true prophet receives the Word as Isaiah did: "Here I am, send me." or Mary: "Be it unto me according to your word."

Terrible disasters may await us. The planet is already sundered by war, starvation, drought, famine, earthquake, flood, tornado. But we should not read too much into these signs. Those who study weather patterns tell us that until a decade ago we had approximately fifty years of extremely unusual weather, fairly temporate and predictable. Now we are back to ordinary weather patterns, violent, and unpredictable. "Why do we bother to listen to the forecast?" we say. "It's almost always wrong." So let us not read an easy eschatology into a return to the kind of weather patterns which have been the norm for our planet during most of recorded history.

Jesus said, remember, that even the angels in heaven do not know the time of his return. No one can prophecy that everything is going to be easy, that there won't be more tornados or hurricanes or volcanic explosions. But nuclear warfare is an ultimate cursing. And we are told to bless.

Zephaniah, after prophesying the terrible things which would result from hardness of heart, then proclaims, "Your God is mightily in your midst. He will exult with joy over you, he will renew you by his love; he will dance with shouts of joy for you as on a day of festival."

The love of God is a great mystery, so far does it transcend our own diminished capacity for love and blessing. The marvel is that God's love can transform and augment ours. As we turn our hearts to blessing, we share in Heaven's blessing.

How do we bless those who would damn? those who would consign most of the world to eternal hell? How do we bless assassins and terrorists, or even the lawyers in the criminal courts who try to get verdicts of not guilty for people they well know to be guilty?

How do I bless the person who is no longer willing to be my friend because of a secret I never told? How do I bless the person who did pass on that secret?

One thing I have learned is that I do not have to do it graciously. A blessing given is a blessing given. I sat in my quiet corner one night after jury duty, the Bible open on my lap, and I knew that I still had hurt in my heart, and that I was still angry at whoever was permitting a great load of blame and shame to be laid on me. And I heard myself saying—and meaning—"Oh, God, bless the bastard."

What did I mean by that? Just what I said. I was not demanding justification, or vindication, or a change of heart on the other person's part. The blessing stood, just as it was.

We must bless without wanting to manipulate. Without insisting that everything be straightened out right now. Without insisting that our truth be known. This means simply turning whoever it is we need to bless over to God, knowing that God's powerful love will do what our own feeble love or lack of it won't. I have suggested that it is a good practice to believe in six impossible things every morning before breakfast, like the White Queen in *Through the Looking Glass*. It is also salutary to bless six people I don't much like every morning before breakfast.

If we all blessed Muammar Qaddafi, what do you suppose would happen?

If a blessing is irrevocable, what about a cursing? We human beings can, and do, hurt each other through cursing. Most of us are aware of the power of black magic and its hexes and spells and killing sticks, and are rightly afraid of and shun it. But the most powerful evil magic is weak before Christ, and shrivels in the light of Christ's love.

The light shines in the darkness, and the darkness cannot put it out.

Then what about all that primitive cursing of our enemies in the Bible? Here again we are pushed to move on beyond the spiritual place where some of the biblical narrators and singers of the psalms stood. God uses raggle taggle material, and there is hope that we will learn from experience. We do not have to invent the lever, the needle, the wheel over and over again. We are not expected to sit still in our understanding, but to add wisdom to knowledge, and to move on.

The vision of God in Genesis is varied, and contradictory. The God we read about in the stories seems often different from the God in the histories, or the laws. God was seen both as the Creator of the universe, and as the tribal God who helped his chosen people take over the neighbour's land. God was the Maker of all the stars, and God was the masculine warrior God. This jealous God commanded that all the foreigners be killed in case his own people became seduced by the neighbouring gods and started worshipping them, him, her, or it—which often happened.

Even with the assertion that the other gods demanded literal blood sacrifice, the command to kill all the people seems forensically bloody. And of course, not all the people did get killed, because we read of many marriages between tribes. Despite the order for slaughter, the people of El Shaddai married the worshippers of other gods, and this angered their anthropomorphic god. It's all pretty primitive because they were, after all, a primitive people.

The contradictory views of God in the early books of Scripture can be confusing—the constant demands to destroy alien nations, the bloodiness of it all. But then there breaks through a shining, as when we read in the tenth chapter of Deuteronomy, "And now, Israel, what does the Lord your God require of you, but to fear the Lord your God, to walk in all his ways, and to love God, and to serve the Lord God with all your heart and with all your soul." And in contradiction to all the demands for bloodshedding, "Love you, therefore, the stranger, for you were strangers in the land of Egypt."

But Deuteronomy was written long after the saga of Jacob, after the giving of the commandments, the setting up of ceremonial laws, the moving into a more forensic way of life. Jacob was not bound by the details of hundreds of laws. He knew that he could not earn God's blessing, but he did not hesitate to demand it. He knew that he needed it. And this deep need and passion showed that his heart had a deeper understanding than his conniving head. If Jacob had had to earn God's love, he would not have gone far.

Nor would he have seen those angels and the wonder of at-one-ment, of knowing the place where he had slept to be a sacred place, the house of God. How often do we feel such wondrous awe? We have lost much of it in the effort to have God as a friend, or, not so much a friend as a pal. And that doesn't work, either. God is both transcendent and immanent, and often in the wondrous moments of sheltering under the eternal wings, we know ourselves and all the stars in all the galaxies as belonging to God. How can we not feel awe?

Oh, I am in awe of the maker of galaxies and geese, stars and starfish, mercury and men (male and female). Sometimes it is rapturous awe; sometimes it is the numinous dread Jacob felt. Sometimes it is the humble awe of knowing that ultimately

I belong to God, to the Maker whose thumb print is on each one of us. And that is blessing.

* * *

Poor Esau. If he felt awe at the glory of the stars we are not told about it. He was more interested in satisfying his immediate hungers. He didn't get much love, either from his mother or his twin brother. But he did not hold grudges. Rebekah told Jacob to go away until Esau cooled off, and she knew her elder son well enough to know that he would indeed cool off. I like that in Esau, the unwillingness to hold on to anger, the lack of desire for revenge. Perhaps Jacob did not know his brother well enough to know that Esau had a generous personality. Despite Rebekah's rank favouritism of the handsome younger son, Esau had fine qualities, including the refusal to sulk and smoulder over past insults.

Even about marriage, Esau did not receive the loving parental advice lavished on Jacob. We read that, "Esau, seeing that the daughters of Canaan did not please Isaac his father," went to Ishmael, his uncle, and married Mahalath, one of Ishmael's daughters. That doesn't seem to have pleased his parents, either. Esau, from the moment of his birth, was given a hard time.

But he did not respond to the indignities heaped upon him with cursing.

Even if I do not feel "good" about it, I must learn to bless and not damn. During a period of discussion at one conference I emphasized this and mentioned, rather casually, that I had said of someone, "God, bless the bastard." Not only did this startle some of the people at the conference, it was also liberating. God loves us as we are, even at our most ungracious. And to bless, no matter how little we may feel like it, is to participate in love.

Cursing is a boomerang. If I will evil towards someone else, that evil becomes visible in me. It is an extreme way of being forensic, toward myself, as well as toward whoever outrages me. To avoid contaminating myself and everybody around me. I must work through the anger and the hurt feelings and the demands for absolute justice to a desire for healing. Healing for myself, and my anger, first, because until I am at least in the process of healing, I cannot heal; and then healing for those who have hurt or betrayed me, and those I have hurt and betrayed. I must hope for healing for those two arrogant men with their clever lawyers; healing for the clever lawyers, too, deliberately defending two men who had used knives with intent to hurt or kill, but who hadn't used them skillfully enough to hurt the old woman they attacked as badly as the assistant district attorney claimed.

Are they any less worthy of blessing than was tricky Jacob? Or you? Or me?

Perhaps most difficult of all is learning to bless ourselves, just as we are. Before we can ask God to bless us, we must be able to accept ourselves as blessed—not perfect, not virtuous, not sinless—just blessed.

If we have to be perfect before we can know ourselves blessed, we will never ask for the transfiguring power of God's love, because of course we are unworthy. But we don't have to be worthy, we just have to acknowledge our need, to cry out, "Help me!" God will help us, even if it's in an unexpected and shocking way, by swooping down on us to wrestle with us. And in the midst of the wrestling we, too, will be able to cry out, "Bless me!"

I am certain that God will bless me, but I don't need to know how. When we think we know exactly how the one who made us is going to take care of us, we're apt to ignore the angel messengers sent us along the way.

There is a story of an old man who lived by a river. In the spring the rains were heavy, and the river rose. The sheriff came by in his jeep, and said to the old man. "The river is going to flood, and I want to evacuate you."

The old man folded his arms confidently. "I have faith in God. God will take care of me."

The sheriff shook his head and drove off.

The river continued to rise. It lapped about the old man's house, rising up to the porch. The sheriff came by in a row boat, and said, "The river is continuing to rise. I really need to evacuate you."

The old man looked at the river which covered his steps and lapped across the porch. He folded his arms. "I have faith in God. God will take care of me."

The sheriff shook his head, and rowed away.

And the river inched higher. At last the old man was clinging to his roof tree. The sheriff came by in a helicopter and hovered above the old man. "I really must evacuate you. You'll drown if I don't."

But the old man repeated, "I have faith in God. God will take care of me."

Frustrated, the sheriff left.

And the river rose even higher. And the old man drowned.

In heaven, he was very upset. He went to God and said, "Why did you do this to me? Why did you let me drown? I kept telling the sheriff that I had faith in you, and that you would take care of me."

God said, "You ninny! I sent you a jeep, and a rowboat, and a helicopter!"

When we ask God for help, we can't insist that help come in the way that we have decided. If we are demanding specific blessings, we may miss the actual ones God has sent to us.

> Bless the Lord, O my soul, and all that is within me, bless
>   his holy Name.
> Bless the Lord, O my soul, and forget not all his benefits.

He forgives all your sins, and heals all your infirmities;
He redeems your life from the grave and crowns you with
 mercy and loving kindness.
The Lord is full of compassion and mercy, slow to anger
 and of great kindness.
For as the heavens are high upon the earth, so is his mercy
 great upon those who fear him.
Bless the Lord, you angels of his, you mighty ones who do
 his bidding, and hearken to the voice of his word.
Bless the Lord, all you his hosts, you ministers of his who
 do his will.
Bless the Lord, all you works of his, in all places of his
 dominion, bless the Lord, O my soul.

St Francis to another friar, on
their way home to the monastery:
"The best thing that could ←
happen is to be refused
entrance and thrown out
into the darkness."

A Sense of Wonder

8

THERE WERE MANY TIMES in Jacob's life when he must have experienced intense loneliness. After he had stolen his father's blessing, with his mother's urging, he could not stay at home to enjoy it, but had to go away, to stay with his uncle Laban.

Is there anybody in the world who has not, at one time or another, experienced a deep loneliness, when all support systems fail, when there is nobody there—nobody? It is at such times that I reach out for God most longingly. Here, as God was present for Jacob, not God Out There, high in a distant heaven, but present, even in the loneliest depths of my heart. For if I cannot find God here, within, how can I find el anywhere else?

Jacob's vision of glory came in the midst of his terror. We do not have to be at peace, or have perfect conditions, in order to glimpse glory. It was as possible for me to have a flash of heavenly understanding in that tiny box of a jury room as in church or out on the grandeur of the ocean.

The universe is immeasurably vast. God only Out There, looking on, does not help me. I seek and know a closer God. God not only within all that has been made, God not only within during the lifetime of Jesus of Nazareth, but God within, right now, within me, in the salt of my tears, the beating of my heart.

Lancelot Andrewes wrote:

Be, O Lord, within me to strengthen me
Without me to guard me
Over me to shelter me,
Beneath me to stablish me
Before me to guide me
After me to forward me
Round about me to secure me.

Those lines were written four centuries ago. The idea of God everywhere is not new, but God has been pushed Out There, without, for so long, that we forget the within-ness, and the marvel that God can come and reveal wonder in the most ordinary things. One early summer day I came home from trying to clip back the weed alders which were blocking the view from the star watching rock, and met a young friend, also returning to the house, carrying his shirt which was stained red with the miracle of tiny, luscious wild strawberries, and which remained pinkly patterned after numerous launderings. This uncovenanted bounty of the field was worth one shirt, and a reminder of the marvellousness of the ordinary loveliness on the hillside by Crosswicks.

Sometimes the loveliness of God's presence comes in the midst of pain.

I wasn't quite over a bad case of shingles when I went south to conduct a retreat. I felt miserable. The shingles blisters, which had managed to get even into my ear, had burst my eardrum.

The weather was not cooperating. Instead of being warm and sunny (I had hoped to be able to sit on the beach and bask in the sun and heal) it was cold, rainy, and raw.

When the rain finally stopped, I went for a silent walk on the beach with two caring friends. The ocean was smothered in fog, but occasionally the curtain lifted enough to reveal a fishing boat, and a glimpse of muted silver on sea. One of my companions found some lovely driftwood. The other picked up some tiny donax shells and put them in my palm. And there, in the silence, in the fog, in my pain, was a sensation of being surrounded by the almighty wings of God, right there, at that time, in that place, God with us.

As Lancelot Andrewes called on God to be.

When I think of Jacob alone, his head on his stone pillow, I can easily hear Lancelot Andrewes' words coming from him. The vision of angels which came to him when he fled from home, and had not yet reached Laban, changed Jacob's perception of God, and he vowed a vow, bargaining with his father's God, but finally affirming,

> *then shall the Lord be my God: and this stone, which I have placed for an altar, shall be God's house: and of all that God shall give me, I will surely give a tenth to God.*

Jacob was in the habit of making bargains: You do this for me, God, and you can be my God. But he was beginning to learn wonder, and awe at the marvel of the vision he had been sent.

How often we are given visions, and walk right by them, or through them (like the old man by the river) because we have lost our sense of wonder, our belief in all that lies on the other side of reason.

On my desk I have a placard which my granddaughter, Charlotte, made for me as a Christmas present, copying out

Shakespeare's words in large italic letters: "Oh, wonderful, wonderful, and most wonderful, and yet again wonderful, and after that out of all whooping."

This delightful gift was a result of a week Charlotte and her sister, Léna spent with us at Crosswicks. In the evening we would get into the big four-poster bed with mugs of cocoa, and read *As You Like It,* taking turns with the roles. Charlotte was reading Celia, one of Shakespeare's most delightful and liberated characters, when she hooted out this joy with a spontaneity and lack of inhibition which we often lose as we move from the childhood world of play and daydreams into the adult world where we have to worry about the price of fuel oil and the rising cost of living. How sad that so often we stifle our sense of joy and wonder.

A letter to me from an eleven-year-old girl posed the question, "How can I remain a child forever and not grow up?"

I wrote back, "I don't think you can, and I don't think it would be a good idea if you could. What you *can* do, and what I hope you *will* do, is remain a child forever, and grow up, too." That is what it means to be a whole human being, rather than an isolated fragment of our own chronology.

Charlotte, Léna, and I, reading *As You Like It,* aloud, were children, and they were also young adolescents, and I was also a grandmother, but we shared our wonder. We culled other quotable lines from the play, chortling as Rosalind says, "Why, know you not that I am a woman? When I think, I must speak!"

Perhaps that's one of the best of the feminine characteristics. When we think, we speak. Which means that we have the courage of our convictions. Sometimes we tell stories, or write stories. Children have not lost the notion, as many adults have, that to read is to speak; it is, in fact, a form of dialogue. That is probably the chief difference between reading a book and watching television. In viewing we do not engage in dialogue; we are acted upon; we do not, in any true creative sense,

What about respond to a subtle joke when there is no canned laughter.

participate. But when we read, we are creators. If the reader cannot create the book along with the writer, then the book is stillborn. The reader is also an artist.

Léna and Charlotte and I were artists as we read aloud.

Rosalind and Celia were universe disturbers in their own inimitable ways, Celia being willing for love of her cousin to go into exile. And because a sense of wonder was vivid in Celia, she was able to make a game of something that was supposed to be humiliating and shameful. And in the end the "wicked uncle," who had sent Rosalind and Celia into exile, repented. The wicked may "play games," but, paradoxically, they do not know how to play.

Abraham Joshua Heschel says that "indifference to the sublime wonder of living" lies behind all the evils which have befallen our sorry century. I remember Léna and Charlotte as little ones twirling with delight in a daisy-filled meadow, singing ring-around-a-rosy with me, until we all fell into the white and green field, breathless with laughter.

Heschel continues, "Modern man fell into the trap of believing that everything can be explained, that reality is a simple affair which only has to be organized in order to be mastered."

I cannot explain angels, nor do I need to. But I want to hear the lovely swish of their wings, to know that they are there, God's messengers of love and hope. — *angels in the sky*

To lose our sense of wonder is to grow rigid, unable to accept change with grace. This has been a century of change, accelerating change, which gives every indication of continuing to accelerate. We tend to adjust to the technological changes fairly well. We're not like the old woman who announced, "If God had wanted us to fly, he wouldn't have created trains."

We're grateful for the advances of medicine. I love the electronic typewriter which is sensitive to my thoughts as they flow through my fingers. Technology's outer changes are very visible, and we've managed to keep up with them fairly well. But we haven't changed inwardly enough to keep up with the changes we've made outwardly, thus creating problems we're just beginning to recognize. Or to refuse to recognize. For if we recognize that our spiritual development lags woefully behind our intellectual development, and that we must do something to heal this brokenness before we are split completely asunder, then we must open ourselves to God. This is dangerous to our self-satisfaction or complacency. If we open ourselves to the untamed God, we may get hurt. We may make mistakes. We may find that our lives are being turned around. And that takes courage, a childlike courage.

We become whole by being all of ourselves, including the aspects of ourselves we like least as well as those of which we are able to approve. When we try to approve of ourselves (rather than to love ourselves) we tend to lose both our senses of humour and of wonder. Only if I retain the irradiating joy as I see the first trout lily in the spring, the first bright red of the partridge berries in the autumn, can I become a "grown-up."

Abraham, Isaac, and Jacob were "grown-ups" in the proper sense. They accepted themselves as they were, and they remained sensitive to the wonder of God. And they were willing to change, to move into new ways.

Not only did Abraham marry Keturah, after Sarah's death, and have children with her, he also (according to the custom of the day) had concubines, and more children by them as he lived out his one hundred threescore and fifteen years.

Did he really? Did the patriarchs live as long as Scripture tells us, or did they count age differently? I'm ready to grant the vast length of their years a willing suspension of disbelief. They lived on a planet as yet unpolluted. Air was clean and fresh to breathe. Rain water was pure and could be tasted with relish; acid rain was many centuries away. Food was simple and wholesome, rough and full of bulk. It is quite likely that people then lived longer than we do, whereas during the Dark and

Middle Ages and for many centuries thereafter they had far shorter life-spans than we have—and by we, I mean those of us in the Western world, for the current life span in the Third World is no longer than the life-span in Europe in the Middle Ages.

Ishmael—Abraham's first son, the little boy dying of thirst in the desert, to whom God gave a spring of water—Ishmael, too, lived to a ripe old age, "a hundred and thirty-seven years," when "he gave up the ghost and died."

A phrase much used in Scripture, to give up the ghost. What does it mean? Ghost = spirit = breath. In the liturgy we ask that our thoughts may be cleansed by the *inspiration* of the Holy Spirit, that the Spirit may breathe truth and renewal into us.

When we give up the spirit, we stop breathing, we give the ghost back to the Creator. When their time came, Abraham and the others of the day gave up the ghost "and were gathered to their fathers."

That was enough. Life was full, and there was little questioning of what came after it. Such questions did not come until a more densely-populated world where the wicked flourished and the innocent suffered and the inequities of this life became more apparent.

"The world has enough for every man's need," said Gandhi, "but not for every man's greed." There are many who will hunger and thirst. But they are never beyond the saving grace of God's love, the tender shepherd who will lift the dying child into strong and gentle arms and say, "Come, little lamb, into my Kingdom."

✳ ✳ ✳

In that desert land wells were so important that they were given names. There was an honouring of the reality of water and stone, of tree and sand. Everything in the created order belonged to God, and what is God's is named.

, I have named many of my favourite pausing places as I walk across the fields and through the woods. I love the Grandfather Oak which somehow survived whatever disease killed off most of the oaks in our part of New England, and who now looks benevolently down on many grandchildren oaklings. There is one ancient maple tree which is known to me as the Icon Tree, and one mountain ash which we discovered one autumn, rising above the scrub cherry and alder, bearing a bright load of berries, and which is for me the Star Singer. One of the favourite anthems we sang in choir was to the melody of the Ash Grove, and we sang the song of the stars in their courses, and hence the name Star Singer for this slender ash tree. There is Cleft Rock (and the two largest clefts were noticeably wider after the earthquake and more difficult to leap across), and the Star Watching Rock and the Precipice.

I like houses to have names, not numbers, but I am told that when the present postmaster here in our village is retired we will no longer be able to use "Crosswicks" as our address, but will, instead, be limited to a number. A house may have a number, but a home has a name.

It is harder to name things in the city. Our apartment building has a number, and is also called the Clebourne, but the Clebourne means little to me; it is, maybe, the old lobby with its marble walls, reminders of a grander day, but it is not the rooms in which we live. Some of the rooms have names, though. The room with the big Morse portrait of my great-grandmother with her harp, and great-great-aunt with her flute, is, logically, the Portrait Room, in which I have my desk, and the Quiet Corner where I sit at night to write in my journal, to read Scripture, to pray.

The city is over-crowded, and Manhattan is an island whose boundaries cannot be widened. There is no way to make room for everybody except by moving up, in taller and more cramped buildings. This crowding is a precursor of violence. I used to have favourite trees and resting places in the Riverside Park, but now I no longer feel safe strolling and relaxing. I go to the park now to walk the dog, and I no longer linger; I walk the dog.

When we first moved back to the city, the dog was Oliver, a collie who appeared in the village, and then in our lives and who, of course, had to make the move to New York with us. After Oliver came Timothy, the Irish Setter. New York has a dog pick-up law, (which maybe half of us dog-walkers observe) and when I put the leash on the dog, I also put a plastic bag in my pocket. Timothy, like all Irish Setters, dropped large, redolent loads, and I picked his up with my hand in the plastic bag, so that my fingers touched nothing except the plastic, and walked along, holding his warm, cereal-scented b.m., and feeling absolutely fearless. Suppose someone came up to me? I'd simply hold out the odorous bag and say, "Yes?"

There came a day which I knew was Timothy's last. He was fifteen-and-a-half years old—extremely old for an Irish Setter—and I think he knew it was dying day. A friend helped me to get him to the animal hospital, driving me there through the city streets, with Timothy lying in my lap, his head against my breast like a trusting baby's. My friend carried him in for me, and while we waited for the vet, again he lay in my lap, not in pain, simply letting the life drain out of him. When we put him on the surgical table there was no question that his time had come. The doctor said to me, "Do you want to see him afterwards?" Not understanding, I replied, "Not particularly. I'll stay with him now."

"I wish you wouldn't," the doctor said. "People tend to get nervous, and that upsets the dog. I'm thinking only of what is best for the dog."

"Then you'll let me stay with him and hold him," I said. I was told later that this city veterinary doctor had had to deal with hysterical people who perhaps loved their dramatics more than their animals. Anyhow, he looked at me, looked at the dog, and let me stay. I held my old friend while the needle was inserted. I was not nervous, but there were tears slipping down my cheeks. I said to the doctor, "I do not think that anyone, animal or human, ought to die without being held."

Timothy was not the first animal I have held through death. Probably he won't be the last. When we take on an animal, we have to accept that a dog's life span is considerably shorter than ours. Now I walk with Doc—Doctor Charlotte Tyler (named after my husband's role, Dr. Charles Tyler), a romping, loving, willful Golden Retriever.

Abraham's sons, Isaac and Ishmael, reconciled at their father's death bed, were with him, and I hope that they held the old man as life ebbed away, their own hands touching.

Ishmael, Scripture tells us, "died in the presence of his brethren," Isaac, and the children of Keturah, and likely the children of Abraham's concubines. Perhaps Isaac held Ishmael, and Laughter eased Bitterness.

Isaac was forty years old when he married Rebekah, and his son, Esau "was forty years old when he took to wife, Judith, the daughter of Beeri the Hittite, and Bashemath, the daughter of Elon the Hittite, which were a grief of mind to Isaac and Rebekah." A grief of mind, not because the women made quite a harem for Esau—having several wives was customary—and also compassionate, since there were many more women than men, and a husbandless woman had a hard time surviving. What upset Isaac and Rebekah was that Judith and Bashemath worshipped alien gods. They would also give Esau more children, and, therefore, strength, if Esau wanted to pay back Jacob for all his trickery.

Esau and Jacob did not have the kind of intimacy often associated with twins. And certainly with their startling physical differences they were obviously fraternal rather than identical twins. Even when they made peace with each other, it may have seemed to Jacob an uneasy truce. It is often more difficult to accept forgiveness than to give it.

The long-gone world of the rival twins was not as different from the world of today as it might seem. We are still struggling with alien gods; we are still trying to learn what it means to forgive and be forgiven.

It is not just that the God of the Christian appears different from the God of the Muslim or the Buddhist, but that even within Christianity God wears so many contradictory aspects that Christianity seems appallingly inconsistent to many people. It is not surprising that Christians themselves (ourselves) have made many people not only mistrustful of Christianity, but anti-Christian.

A brilliant young professor, whose son had recently joined a rigid, orthodox Jewish sect in Jerusalem, where all questions were given final answers, all actions dictated, said bitterly, "Religion is divisive." I have to agree that yes, alas, it is. But we were together in saying that God is not. Religion is divisive when it becomes fanaticism—an insistence that we know all the answers, and that anybody whose answers differ from ours is damned.

The human being's attempt to understand the Creator can never be final, but dynamic, in motion, almost as though we were climbing that ladder of angels joining heaven and earth.

Do we get dizzy on the ladder? Refuse to climb? Turn over and tell the vision to go away?

One of J.B. Phillips' books is entitled, *Your God is too Small.* Our God becomes too small when we make God in our own image, instead of heeding the image of God in us. In us, not outside us, but in us, waiting to be recognized.

Our call, no matter what our vocation, is to witness to the God within, the God who is One.

Cardinal Suhard writes, "To be a witness does not consist in engaging in propaganda, nor even in stirring people up, but in being a living mystery. It means to live in such a way that one's life would not make sense if God did not exist."

My faith in God, who is eternally loving and constant even as my understanding grows and changes, makes life not only worth living, but gives me the courage to dare to disturb the universe when that is what el calls me to do. Sometimes simply being open, refusing to settle for finite answers, disturbs the universe. Questions are disturbing, especially those which may threaten our traditions, our institutions, our security. But questions never threaten the living God, who is constantly calling us, and who affirms for us that love is stronger than hate, blessing stronger than cursing.

If our planet is frequently dark, it may be Lucifer's bitter breath blowing against the light—Lucifer, the prototypical anti-universe disturber, wanting the glory for himself, instead of rejoicing in being the most luminous of all the lightbearers.

It is easy to name myriad anti-universe disturbers. We have them in our own country. What confuses us is that people can simultaneously disturb the universe both creatively *and* destructively. Some of the greatest advances in medicine, which not only save human life, but improve its quality, have come about because of our blasting open the heart of the atom. The laser can be used to save lives and also as a terrible instrument of destruction. Almost everything the human being has made, from plastic to penicillin, can be an instrument of both good and evil.

We daily have to make choices between good and evil, and it is not always easy, or even possible, to tell the difference between the two. Whenever we make a choice of action, the first thing to ask ourselves is whether it is creative or destructive. Will it heal, or will it wound? Are we doing something to make ourselves look big and brave, or because it is truly needed? Do we know the answers to these questions? Not always, but we will never know unless we ask them. And we will never dare to ask them if we close ourselves off from wonder.

When I need a dose of wonder I wait for a clear night and go look for the stars. In the city I see only a few, but only a few are needed. In the country the great river of the Milky Way streams across the sky, and I know that our planet is a small part of that river of stars, and my pain of separation is healed.

Dis-aster makes me think of dis-grace. Often the wonder of the stars is enough to return me to God's loving grace.

Breaking the Taboo

9

THE STORY OF JACOB'S AND RACHEL'S LOVE reads like a fairy tale. Rebekah became Isaac's bride without trial or trouble. Not so with Jacob and Rachel. No prince in a fairy tale had more trouble in marrying his princess than did Jacob.

It started out, in the usual way by a desert well, where Rachel came with her father's sheep, to give them water.

> *Jacob saw Rachel, and went near and rolled the stone away from the well's mouth, and watered the flock of Laban, his mother's brother. And Jacob kissed Rachel, and lifted up his voice and wept. And Jacob told Rachel that he was her father's brother, and that he was Rebekah's son, and she ran and told her father.*

Why did Jacob weep? With joy? Men wept freely before too much "civilization" taught them that tears are unmanly. But

Jacob was sure enough of his own manhood that he was free to do all kinds of things which would be frowned on today. It's a freedom we all need to regain, and surely men are as much in need of liberation as women. Their chains are perhaps less visible, but easily as crippling.

Jacob wept.

He was exhausted, fleeing for his life, leaving the known safety of home. And there at the well was a beautiful young woman, and he learned that she was Rachel, and he loved her, and wept.

> So Jacob told Rachel who he was, and Rachel ran and told her father, and Laban ran to meet Jacob, and kissed him, and brought him to his house. And Jacob stayed with Laban for a month.
>
> Then Laban said, "Surely you should not serve me for nothing. Tell me, what shall your wages be?"
>
> Now Laban had two daughters, and the elder daughter was Leah, and she was tender-eyed, while Rachel, the younger, was beautiful, and well-favoured. Jacob loved Rachel, and said to Laban, "I will serve you for seven years for Rachel, your younger daughter."
>
> Laban agreed, and Jacob served him for seven years, which seemed to him just a few days, for the love he had for Rachel. Then Jacob said, "Give me my wife, for I have fulfilled my seven years. Give me my wife that I may go in unto her."
>
> So Laban made a great wedding feast.

And that evening Laban took Leah to Jacob, instead of Rachel. The trickster was out-tricked in an extraordinary fashion. And here we must give the fairy tale an enormous suspension of disbelief. Even if Jacob had wined and dined extremely well at the wedding feast, it is hard to believe that he wouldn't have noticed that he was making love with Leah, and not with his beloved Rachel. But, according to the story, he did not notice the exchange until morning, and then he cried out to Laban,"What is this that you have done to me? Did I not serve with you for Rachel? Why have you tricked me?"

Laban said, "In our country we must not give the younger in marriage before the first born."

So after marrying Leah, Jacob also married Rachel, and agreed to serve Laban another seven years for her.

It was Rachel Jacob loved, not Leah, and these things happen. We do not always choose those to whom we respond with love. From the moment he saw her at the well, Jacob loved Rachel, not Leah. However, Leah was his number one wife according to the custom of the time, and he lived with her as his wife, and she conceived, and bore a son, and called his name Reuben, for she said, "Surely the Lord has looked upon my affliction; now, therefore, my husband will love me."

But it's never that easy. Nor was it any easier for Rachel, because she did not conceive. Jacob's love of her could not fill her empty womb. Meanwhile, Leah bore three more sons, Simeon, Levi, and Judah, and with each one she continued to hope that Jacob would come to love her. One wife had his children; one had his love.

Barren Rachel envied Leah, her older sister, saying to Jacob, "Give me children, or I will die." This made Jacob angry with Rachel and he said, "Am I in God's place, who has withheld from you the fruit of the womb?"

Then Rachel did what her grandmother-in-law, Sarah, had done before her; she gave her maid, Bilhah, to Jacob, saying, "She shall bear upon my knees, that I may also have children by her."

Bilhah conceived, twice, and bore two sons, Dan and Naphtali.

When Leah realized that she was through conceiving, she,

in her turn, gave Zilpah, her maid, to Jacob, and Zilpah bore Gad and Asher. (How must the maids have felt, being offered to another woman's husband, like it or not, to bear children for their mistresses? It was customary; must it not also have been humiliating?)

We know more about Hagar, Ishmael's mother, than we do about Bilhah and Zilpah, but they each bore two sons who were among the twelve sons of Jacob who made up the twelve tribes of Israel.

Reuben, who must have been an adolescent by the time Gad and Asher were born, went out into the fields at the time of the wheat harvest, and found mandrakes, which he brought to his mother, Leah. The mandrake was supposed to have magic powers, and its root to resemble the human form. I think of Donne's lines,

> *Go and catch a falling star,*
> *Get with child a mandrake root.*

Rachel wanted her sister's mandrakes, and asked for them, and Leah, rather understandably, refused. "Isn't it enough for you that you have taken my husband from me? Would you also take away my son's mandrakes?"

Rachel said, "Then Jacob shall lie with you tonight for your son's mandrakes."

So when Jacob came in from the fields, Leah was the one who met him. And he lay with her that night, and she conceived, and bore a fifth son, Issachar. And she conceived again, and had a sixth son, Zebulon. After that she had a daughter, Dinah.

And God "remembered Rachel," Scripture says, and she conceived, and bore a son, and said, "God has taken away my reproach," and she called her son Joseph.

After the birth of Joseph, Jacob went to Laban and said, "Send me away, that I may go to my own place, and to my own country. Give me my wives and my children, for whom I have served you all these years."

Laban did not want to let Jacob go, because under Jacob's care, Laban's flocks had multiplied greatly. Finally he asked, "What shall I give you?"

Jacob answered. "You shall not give me anything. But I will go through your flock today, and remove all the speckled and spotted cattle, goats, and sheep."

Jacob would be allowed to keep the less desirable beasts as his reward for his years of service with his father-in-law, leaving for Laban the purer animals.

But Jacob was up to his tricks again, this time with an early example of genetic engineering, breeding the speckled and spotted animals for strength so that they became more desirable than the others.

Laban was not pleased, and Jacob saw his father-in-law's displeasure in his countenance. So he quickly gathered together his wives and maids and children and set them on camels, and he stole away with all his goods and all his spotted cattle, fleeing once again because his trick had been found out.

Laban, unaware that Jacob and Rachel were running away from him, went to shear his sheep, when he discovered that his teraphim had been stolen. Household gods, as the Romans later called them.

When Laban discovered that Jacob and Rachel and Leah were gone, along with his images, he rushed after them.

Jacob had pitched his tent on Mount Gilead, and there Laban overtook him.

"What have you done!" Laban cried, "that you left without telling me, and carried away my daughters as though they were captives you had won in battle? . . . Why have you stolen my gods?"

Jacob admitted to Laban that he had run away because he was afraid. His very willingness to acknowledge his fear was a sign of his courage. And cunning. But he denied taking Laban's teraphim, and suggested that his father-in-law search for these small images, swearing, rashly, that whoever had them should not live—a kind of cursing for which he would pay bitterly. For he was unaware that it was his beloved Rachel who had taken the teraphim, perhaps for protection during their flight, perhaps because they were the familiar little gods she was accustomed to. Jacob, unknowing, called for the death of whoever had stolen the images. Was this curse irrevocable, as blessings are irrevocable? Did Jacob's rash words cause Rachel to die in giving birth to her second son, Benjamin?

Laban looked through Jacob's tent, and through Leah's tent, and then he went into Rachel's tent.

> *Now Rachel had taken the images, and put them in the camel's furniture and sat on them ... And Rachel said to her father, "Let it not displease my lord that I cannot stand to greet you, because the custom of women is upon me." And Laban searched, but he did not find the images.*

The custom of women. The menstrual period. Blood.

Blood, the great taboo of the Old Testament. A woman during her menstrual period was thought to be unclean, because to shed blood is to shed life.

This attitude still prevails in some parts of the world today. I stood outside a Jain temple in Bombay and read the sign out front with its various prohibitions: *Do not enter with shoes on. Women in menstrual cycle not allowed.*

After walking on the filth of any city street, my own New York included, taking off one's shoes seems sensible indeed. But *blood?*

What is there about blood? I started reading an interesting and challenging article by an Islamic scholar. As I read, I was amazed at how completely I was able to accept all that he was saying, and I applauded internally when he affirmed that of course God is female as well as male—and of course women are just as important as men in the eyes of God—except during the menstrual period when women do not say the prayers.

At this point I closed the article. What kind of equality is this? What is there about this blood which is so terrifying to men?

I had cause to learn a good deal about blood this summer, and it has made a great difference in my response to this fluid which, to the ancient Hebrew, was taboo because it represented life itself.

* ✳ *

It began in July when Hugh and I spent fifteen days on a fifty-foot boat with friends in the coastal waters of northwest Canada, near Prince Rupert Island and the Queen Charlotte Islands. There were six of us on the boat, and we were the crew. What there was to be done, the six of us did. We each took our turn on watch. Whoever was at the wheel needed someone else sitting right there on a stool, for drift watch, for in those far northern Canadian waters there are many drifting logs and "dead heads" difficult to see, which could do great damage to a small boat.

Hugh and I were not quite prepared for the vastness of the wilderness, and our almost total isolation. At night we would pull into an inlet, and anchor. Our only companions were seals, dolphins, loons. We saw bear tracks, though we never saw bears themselves. There was usually at least one great eagle perched watchfully high up on a tree in these climactic forests—forests which have grown as much as they can grow.

During those fifteen days and nights of the trip we never saw the moon or the stars; we were so far north that it was still daylight when we went to bed. We learned a lot of wilderness lore, and we ate almost entirely out of the sea. I never thought I'd take having a shrimp or crab cocktail every evening for granted. We caught more than we could eat. We had red snapper and rock fish, and we harvested abalone at low tide, and ate them thinly sliced in garlic butter. We ate the eggs of the sea cucumber. We learned that six people living together in a small amount of space with no privacy, no way to get away from each other, have to practice great forbearance, and maintain an acute sense of humour.

It was a good time, a special time. But there was an unsuspected serpent as there usually is in Eden. Our drinking water was put into the boat whenever we docked near a town, and in one batch of water was an organism known as *aeromonas*. It gets into the human intestine where it does very nasty things. Aeromonas is rare on the north American continent. It is usually found in Australia, almost entirely in the intestines of children where it is self-limiting and short lived. For an adult to be taken over by this little organism is unusual indeed, and in an adult the effects can be quite violent.

It didn't bother anybody else, but for some reason it got me. It invaded my intestines and wrought havoc. Not much is known about it in adults, except that it produces the symptoms of acute ulcerative colitis, and this means pain, severe cramping, and blood. Not unlike the dysentery which afflicted the English in India.

The people at the lab were absolutely delighted to have discovered their second aeromonas, the first having been in a child. My doctor had happened to read an article about aeromonas in *The Lancet,* the English medical journal; he also knew I had been in estuary waters, the only place aeromonas is found, and put two and two together.

It was a relief to have a name to put to my problem, but it didn't put an end to it. Basically, I lost August, spending it in bed. I was weak, tired, and in pain. At night when the pain kept me from sleeping, I listened to tapes, music, and then a series of tapes from a conference at Aqueduct Center in North

Carolina, conducted by Drs. Paul and Margaret Brand. The Brands were both children of Baptist missionaries in India, and were missionaries themselves. They have given their lives to caring for lepers, first in India, and finally in Carville, Louisiana. Dr. Margaret Brand is an opthalmologist, Dr. Paul Brand an orthopaedic surgeon. I listened to their tapes, at first rather reluctantly, because for this cradle Anglican there is something a little uncomfortable about some of the Baptist ways of speaking about God. But as I listened, night after night, I began to feel that I was in the presence of holy people. I was ready to listen when Paul Brand began to speak about the marvellousness of pain.

The most terrible thing to happen to the leper is the loss of pain. The hands and feet of the leper become useless stumps not because of leprosy, but because the leper feels no pain. If the leper loses fingers or toes, as so often happens, it is not because of the disease itself, but because the leper is not warned by pain that the fingers or toes are being hurt, and therefore damage or infection are not prevented. Pain is an angel to tell us that something is wrong. The body which cannot feel pain suffers terrible and often fatal injury.

My body knew pain, and I was doing something about it, taking antibiotics to kill the aeromonas virus, and finally heavy doses of steroids to mitigate the colitis symptoms. Had I had no pain it is quite possible that the little aeromonas could have finished me off. But I had pain, and this pain was alleviated and put in perspective as I listened to Paul Brand rhapsodizing about its wonderful function.

Other marvellous and unexpected insights were given me during those long nights. Blood. It is a scary thing to see the bowl bright with your own red blood. So I was ready and able to listen when, during the small hours of one night, Paul Brand talked about blood.

My husband left his southern Baptist background when he

went away to college. We're both turned off by hymns about being washed in the blood of the Lamb. It sounds too graphic, too literal, to be for me a valid image.

Bleeding, blood, is seen as the source of life, especially for the Jew, for whom the eating of blood is the one real taboo. When God made the new covenant with Noah, after the flood waters subsided, and told him to repopulate the earth, Noah was given only one prohibition: "But flesh with the life thereof, which is the blood thereof, you shall not eat." This prohibition against the consumption of blood is repeated throughout the Bible, loudly, clearly, emphatically. Blood stands for life; that is why an animal must be completely drained of blood before it can be eaten.

Once my husband naively went into a kosher butchershop in our neighbourhood in New York and asked for a leg of lamb, and the poor butcher nearly fainted. Jacob himself added a new taboo the night he wrestled with the angel. The angel smote him on the thigh, and Jacob limped thereafter, so that for Jews ever since, the thigh of the animal, with the sciatic nerve, is prohibited. But the chief taboo is blood.

So, when I was losing blood, I was very aware that I was also losing life. Paul Brand reiterated that the taboo against blood is the strongest taboo in the Bible.

We find mention of this ancient prohibition even in the Psalms. "But they that run after another god shall have great trouble. Their drink offerings of blood will I not offer."

So when Jesus said, in John's gospel,

"Truly, truly, I say to you, unless you eat of the flesh of the Son of man and drink his blood, you have no life in you; he who eats my flesh and drinks my blood has eternal life, and I will raise him up at the last day. For my flesh is food indeed, and my blood is drink indeed. He who eats my flesh and drinks my blood abides in me, and I in him. As the living Father sent me, and I live because of the Father, so he who eats me will live because of me. This is the bread which came down from heaven, not such as the fathers ate and died; he who eats this bread will live forever."

This he said in the synagogue, as he taught at Capernaum.

Many of his disciples, when they heard it, said, "This is a hard saying; who can listen to it?"

But Jesus, knowing in himself that his disciples murmured at it, said to them, "Do you take offense at this?" Then what if you were to see the Son of man ascending where he was before? It is the spirit that gives life, the flesh is of no avail; the words that I have spoken to you are spirit and life. But there are some of you that do not believe." For Jesus knew from the first who those were that did not believe, and who it was that should betray him. And he said, "This is why I told you that no one can come to me unless it is granted him by the Father."

After this many of his disciples drew back and no longer went about with him.

Drink my blood? Break the great taboo? What a shocker that is! For me it was a salutary shock, reminding me that Jesus almost never did what was expected of him, and that God, at all times, and in countless ways, is ready to shock and surprise us into seeing things in a new way. This new understanding about blood is very much with me at communion when I receive the cup. It is indeed a new commandment.

Was it because of the shock of this command of Jesus' that in the Roman Catholic Church until very recently the priest was the only one to drink from the cup, and the people received the bread only? Was it too strong, too shocking? Now, in many Roman Catholic churches, the cup is offered, too. But I don't want ever to take it for granted. I want to be reminded what an extraordinary thing I am doing.

Yet I still find it hard to think of being washed in the blood of the Lamb.

Jesus, little lamb, meek and mild. Jesus, tender shepherd. All right, these are images which have given comfort to countless suffering people. But there is also Jesus, the great Shocker.

Think of the story of the woman with the issue of blood. It has long been one of my favourite stories of the healing power of Jesus—the anguished, bleeding woman trying to reach for the hem of his garment, seeking for the help doctors had been unable to give her (and she had gone to many doctors). Without seeing her, Jesus knew that someone had touched him, because he felt that "virtue" had drained from him.

"Who touched me?" he asked.

The disciples, not understanding, wanted to know how he could ask such a question, with a mob pressing all around him. But the woman crawled forward and confessed that it was she who had touched him, and he told her, lovingly, that her faith had made her whole.

Again he had done something terribly shocking. He had broken the great taboo. The woman with the issue of blood was a woman whose menstrual bleeding had gone on and on without ceasing. She was unclean, and anybody who touched her, or was touched by her, was ritually unclean, and had to go through the prescribed purification procedures, according to the law, before touching anybody else.

So Jesus healed this unclean woman, and by her touch he became ritually unclean himself. He was on his way to the house of Jairus, whose daughter was mortally ill. But Jesus did not stop to follow the law, to purify himself. Ritually unclean, so that anybody who touched him was also unclean, he went to Jairus's house, and raised the little girl from the dead. Thereby he broke another taboo, going against the proscription against touching a dead body. He touched her, and she was alive, and he suggested that she be given food. Shocking behaviour. Everybody he touched, after being touched by the woman with the issue of blood, was unclean. But he brought a dead child back to life, making himself doubly unclean, and the child, also. Ritually unclean, but alive! Jesus acted on the law of love, not legalism. As far as we know, he never did anything about getting himself ritually cleansed. Because love, not law, is the great cleanser. In obeying this higher law he shocked everybody, including his closest friends, in his extraordinary and unacceptable ways of acting out love. Of being Love.

Jesus never broke the law simply to break the law, never as an act of rebellion, but always to obey the higher law of love. That is the only valid reason for breaking the law. Does it violate the law of love? Truly? Then it may be broken, even if it shocks the establishment as Jesus shocked the establishment by healing on the Sabbath, by letting his disciples pluck grain, by reminding us that the Sabbath was made for man, not man for the Sabbath. But his violation of the great blood taboo was the most shocking of all.

✳ ✳ ✳

When Paul Brand was a child, he often went into tiny villages with his father who, although not a doctor himself, often had to lance people's ugly infections to drain them of pus and blood. The young Paul was put off by this. He did not want to become a doctor because he did not like blood.

God has ways of sending us strong messages, without tampering with our free will. In order to become a missionary, Paul Brand had to take a thorough course in first aid. There would be many times when he, like his father, would be in places where there was no doctor. He would have to learn something.

Part of the first aid course was a stint as an orderly in a large London hospital. One night, shortly after he had gone on duty, a young accident victim was brought in. She looked dead.

White, bloodless. There was great rushing around, and a blood transfusion was started. Paul Brand was asked to stay by the woman and to let the nurses know when the blood in the transfusion bag got low.

And so, he said, he watched a miracle. First a tiny flush of colour came into the cheeks. Then the dead white lips were touched with pink. The girl's eyelids fluttered, and she opened her eyes. Blood was indeed life.

So Paul Brand became a doctor, with an entirely new concept of blood. Blood as life. Our life. Our life given to us in the blood and the body. And suddenly he saw all the exhortations to wash in the blood of the lamb not to be literal, as he first took them. Instead, he tells of it as an inner, not an outer washing, and likens it to the life-giving quality of a blood transfusion. He said that if people knew as much about the human body as we do today, they would not have said, "wash me in the blood of the Lamb," but "transfuse me with the blood of the Lamb."

So, when we receive Communion, we are transfused.

Sometimes it is spiritual pain which makes us aware that we need a transfusion. Just as physical pain is a marvel for the human body, an early warning system, so is spiritual pain. So is grief. Grief for the loss of someone we love, either by death, or by broken relationship, which can be more painful than death. Grief is a pain warning.

I grieved for the friendship broken when I was accused of breaking a confidence. And once I was able to grieve, rather than to be angry, and sorry for myself, and to want justice done, then healing became possible, healing which cannot occur without love.

If I was innocent in this case, surely there have been other times in my life when inadvertently I *have* broken confidences. We all say more than we ought to say, or more than we know we have said. Or we don't speak out when a word would make all the difference. Not one of us is totally innocent in either the words of our mouths or the meditations of our hearts. We are all part of this battered, bleeding bride, struggling to regain beauty and purity. And there is nothing, nothing but a transfusion of love which will make any difference at all.

But we need our pain warnings before we can turn to love.

If we watch television, read magazines, we come across a very different attitude toward pain. Avoid it. Deaden it. Take a pill, kill it, then you won't heed its warning. What do the media want us to believe in? Aspirin. Tylenol. Excedrin. Codeine. Or any of the other hard-selling pain-killers. Anything but pain.

We don't want pain. We certainly don't go looking for it. But when it comes, we should heed its warning. I was not offered pain-killers while I was struggling to get rid of the aeromonas. But listening to the music, and to the talking tapes was as effective as a narcotic would have been, and possibly even more so.

A young woman told me of a terrible eye injury for which she could be given no pain-killers, because they would impede the healing of the eye. So, she said, she lay on the floor, writhing in pain, and asked her husband to play records, loud music, Beethoven and Brahms symphonies. And while she was being transfused by music, washed in the great orchestras, the pain subsided until she could lie still, listening. And slowly her eye healed.

There are times when it is appropriate to use pain-killers, as I know through personal experience. Pain is not romantic, and I don't want to suggest sentimentally that it is never intolerable. James Herriot, the Yorkshire veterinarian, writes in one of his books about being called by a farmer to tend a sick animal. Nearby in her stall a cow lay bellowing in mortal pain. The farmer refused to let the vet touch the cow, saying she was going to die, anyhow, and he wasn't going to waste money on her. Herriot could not stand the poor animal's agony, and when the farmer wasn't looking, he took a hypodermic needle and gave the cow a massive shot to assuage her pain so that at least she could die quietly. The next day when he returned to the farm to tend the other animal, he expected a dead cow, but there she was, peacefully munching hay. The painkiller had relaxed her anguish so that she was able to heal.

As usual, there are no valid generalities about pain. But I suspect we need medication less often than the media would have us believe. Sometimes healing and pain can work together to mend us. I don't envy those who have never known any pain, physical or spiritual, because I strongly suspect that the capacity for pain and the capacity for joy are equal. Only those who have suffered are able to rejoice.

It is only when we know ourselves wounded, know that we have lost blood, that we are aware that we need a transfusion. (Sometimes it is only the wise physician who recognizes pain that is intractable, as the Yorkshire vet recognized it, and knows that help is needed.) The transfusion is for someone who has experienced the warning wonder of pain, and the acceptance of the loss of blood, either physically or spiritually.

There are days when I go to the altar and I am less aware of my need for a transfusion than I am on other days. That is all right. But I am always aware that I am tapping into the source of a tremendous power of love. It is not a magic power. As far as I am concerned the experts can worry about words such as transubstantiation. When you need a blood transfusion you don't worry about things like that. The transfusion of love is not always a comfortable one, because such love may push me into letting go some cozy ideas, push me into a new way of looking at God, and therefore at myself.

What am I looking for? Sometimes God opens my eyes so that I see something totally unexpected, something which may cause pain and loss. And then I need to be transfused.

This is always a reminder that God loves us, just as we are.

We don't have to perfect ourselves by adherence to the letter of the law. Jesus has broken the law, radically, with his violation of the taboo of blood, and in the breaking of the taboo has shown the healing power of love. We, too, violate the taboo, break the law. We must understand that when we take the bread and wine we are doing something shocking.

Jesus was not shocked by the woman who was ritually unclean, or the man who collected taxes for the Romans, or even the woman taken in adultery. But he was shocked and grieved by hardness of heart.

We are blessed indeed to be able to feel pain, our body's warning system that something is wrong, and that we need help. Indeed, yes, I need to be washed in the blood of the Lamb, transfused with the blood of the Lamb, for that gives life, and life abundantly.

Let
the Baboons
Clap Their Hands
10

LABAN NEVER FOUND HIS HOUSEHOLD GODS; Rachel was too cunning for him. Had she learned this from her husband?

Jacob (feeling guilty about his genetic manipulation?) was immediately angry with the one he had tricked, and he said to Laban,

> *What is my trespass? What is my sin, that you have followed me so hotly? You have searched all my stuff, and what have you found that belongs to you? I've been with you for twenty years,*

he continued, reminding Laban that his flocks and worldly goods had flourished under Jacob's care.

> *I served you fourteen years for your two daughters, and six years for your cattle, and you have changed my wages ten times.*

They quarreled elegantly in those days, and made up elegantly, too. Jacob and Laban made a covenant, and Jacob set up another stone for a pillar, and called the place by several names, including Mizpah, for, Laban said,

> *The Lord watch between me and thee, when we are absent from one another.*

The word *Mizpah* has often been etched on pins and lockets, and given by lovers to each other. But it was said first by a father-in-law to his son-in-law after they had had a bitter quarrel. After that,

> *Jacob went his way, and the angels of God went with him.*

Did the angels of God remind him that he had unfinished business with his brother, Esau? Jacob sent messengers to Esau, telling them,

> *Thus shall you speak to my lord Esau: his servant, Jacob, says, "I have stayed with Laban until now, and I have oxen, asses, flocks, menservants and womenservants, and I have sent to tell my lord Esau, that I may find grace in his sight."*
>
> *And the messengers returned to Jacob, saying, "We came to your brother, Esau, and he is coming to meet you, with four hundred men."*

This terrified Jacob, because he thought that Esau, after all these years, was coming out to kill him, and he divided his retinue, all the people and all the animals, into two camps, saying,

> *If Esau comes to one company and smites it, then the other will escape. (In his fear, he continued to punish himself for his own trickery.)*

Then he turned to God and said, "O God of my father Abraham, and God of my father Isaac . . . Deliver me from the hand of my brother, for I fear him, lest he come and kill me, and the mothers and their children. And yet it was you, Lord, who said, I will surely do good for you, and make your seed as the sand on the seashore, which cannot be numbered."

Jacob stayed where he was that night, and prepared presents (bribes?) for Esau: two hundred she-goats, twenty he-goats, two hundred ewes, twenty rams, thirty milk camels and their colts, forty kine, and ten bulls, and twenty she-asses, and ten foals.

He did not know his brother very well, our too-clever Jacob. He took his own two wives, and the two womanservants, and his eleven sons, and sent them all over the brook with everything that he had, so that he was alone, completely alone.

And then came the angel to wrestle with him.

Long before, on his flight to Laban, Jacob had seen the ladder of angels, connecting heaven and earth; now he was wrestling with heaven in Person.

And Jacob was left alone; and a man wrestled with him until the breaking of the day. When the man saw that he did not prevail against Jacob, he touched the hollow of his thigh; and Jacob's thigh was put out of joint as he wrestled with him. Then he said, "Let me go, for the day is breaking."

But Jacob said, "I will not let you go, unless you bless me."

And he said to him, "What is your name?"

And he said, "Jacob."

Then he said, "Your name shall no more be called Jacob, but Israel, for you have striven with God and with men, and have prevailed."

Then Jacob asked him, "Tell me, I pray, your name."

But he said, "Why is it that you ask my name?" And

there he blessed him. So Jacob called the name of the place Peniel, saying, "For I have seen God face to face, and yet my life is preserved." The sun rose upon him as he passed Peniel, limping because of his thigh. Therefore to this day the Israelites do not eat the sinew of the hip which is upon the hollow of the thigh, because he touched the hollow of Jacob's thigh on the sinew of the hip.

Jacob's angel wrestled with him all night. We don't always have the courage to keep it up as long as that, though night is often a time for the most intense spiritual struggle, and we don't always know who started it—we, with our unanswerable questions, or the angel, leaping on us unexpectedly.

Perhaps we need the angel to start grappling with us, to turn us aside from the questions which have easy answers to those which cause us to grow, no matter how painful that growth can be.

Luci Shaw condenses into this small poem some of the intense personal longing that was Jacob's, and is ours, in grappling with heaven:

With Jacob

inexorably I cry
as I wrestle
for the blessing,
thirsty, straining
for the joining
till my desert throat
runs dry.
I must risk
the shrunken sinew
and the laming
of his naming

till I find
my final quenching
in the hollow
of the thigh.

This was a critical point, a watershed in Jacob's life, when he came to grips with God—with the reality of heaven itself.

In the Bible, heaven is described metaphorically, not literally. We are given some hints and clues, but it remains for us a realm of mystery.

When my father died when I was seventeen, I pondered heaven and God's plan for el's complex and contradictory children, and it seemed to me evident that nobody I knew, certainly including myself, was ready for heaven after this mortal life in which we are all, one way or another, bent and broken. There may be a handful of people who are prepared for the unveiled vision of God. But most of us are not, most of us still have a vast amount to learn. I don't know how God plans to teach me all that I need to know before I am ready for the Glory, but my faith is based on the belief that I don't have to know. I have to know only that the Maker is not going to abandon me when I die, is not going to make creatures who are able to ask questions which simply cannot be answered in this life, and then drop them with the questions still unanswered.

"But the church says . . ." I am sometimes reminded.

The church (of all denominations) has often said one thing, and then gone on to say something else again. The church pronounced that the earth is flat, that it is the center of creation and God's concern, with the sun and the moon and the stars revolving around us, all for our benefit. It is now generally acknowledged that the earth is part of a solar system on the outskirts of an ordinary spiral galaxy.

Within this century the church said that God is impassible and cannot suffer or grieve or feel pain. It is now generally acknowledged that God, rather than being aloof and impervious, is more like the suffering servant of Isaiah. God is in the desert with the starving children, is in the burning buildings, is present with the piles of bodies in the battletorn cities, a Maker who is part of all that happens and who suffers whenever the creature suffers.

As to who goes to heaven, there seems to be considerable division. Some churches are holding adamantly to a heaven for Christians only. Other churches are asking questions, wondering if this judgmental (if not forensic) attitude toward heaven is true to the love of God.

After Gandhi's death a friend of his was asked whether or not Gandhi was a Christian. The friend replied that the answer depended on what was meant by the question. If the question meant whether Gandhi belonged to one of the established institutions or not, then the answer was no. But if what was meant by the question was whether or not Gandhi believed in Jesus Christ, then the answer was yes.

Once when I was lecturing at a denominational college I was asked, during the question and answer period, whether or not I thought Gandhi was in heaven. "Yes," I said. "But," protested the young man who asked me, "Gandhi did not accept Jesus as his personal Saviour." Didn't he? In any case, when Gandhi attempted to go to a Christian church, he was turned away because he was the wrong colour. The Christian establishment was hardly offering him a Christ of universal love.

It became evident that this young man was far more interested in keeping Gandhi out of heaven than in getting him in. Finally I said, "For me, Gandhi is a Christ figure. I'll be perfectly happy to go wherever he goes. If you want to call that hell, that's your problem."

There is still room for change, change in us all. But we really haven't gone much further than the ancient Egyptians in thinking about the afterlife.

Hugh and I spent two intense weeks in Egypt last winter, with a small group—nine of us—and an excellent Egyptologist, travelling from Cairo and the pyramids and the Sphinx to Luxor, taking a small boat that followed a thousand miles, and penetrated back more thousands of years, on the still largely-unexplored Nile, and on to Aswan and Abu Simbel. We steeped ourselves in the world of ancient Egypt, a world we know about largely because of the Pharaonic faith in God—or the gods. We were filled with awe as we walked through the sacred spaces of the temples, through long, pillared halls to the altar and the holiest holy places.

My heart lifted with wonder at the searching soul of the human being, striving toward God, yearning for the Creator, for the power of love which made all the galaxies and all the solar systems, the Creator of all, for whom the life of our planet is no more than the flicker of an eye.

And it came to me as I stood on the desert sand, looking at the Great Pyramid, that what any civilization says about God tells us more about that civilization than it does about God. Nothing we say about the Creator can begin to be adequate. It is always small and fumbling and human and anthropomorphic—no matter how mighty our monuments.

What those ancient Egyptians were saying to me in their frescoes and carvings was that life would have meant nothing to them at all without their faith in God, even if their gods frequently came to them in both animal and human form.

Were they aware that human beings, marvellous as we are, are also fragile and fragmented? It would seem so, as we studied the complex patterns of their civilization, at least as aware as we are. It seems ironic that the people who refuse to admit any brokenness in themselves are often unhappy. Even if they announce that they are not broken, they still fail to live up to the model of perfection they have set for themselves, a dislocation which produces in them a deep unhappiness. We live most comfortably and lovingly with ourselves when we can look at our brokenness, physical or spiritual, know that God will help us, and that we are loved just as we are. God loves me with all my volatility, stubbornness, flaring temper, clumsiness, and that makes it possible for me to accept myself, loving myself in God's love of me. It also makes it more possible for me to love other people as they are, and not set impossible standards which they cannot meet.

Jesus had visibly imperfect people as friends—a tax collector, a woman who had been possessed of seven demons, a Pharisee who dared speak with him only in the cover of darkness. Where Jesus leads, it is easier for us to follow.

Christ, the second person of the Trinity, was revealed to us in Jesus of Nazareth in an incredible act of love. But Christ can speak to me in other ways, too, ways which do not diminish my love of Jesus as Lord. Christ spoke to me through the ancient culture of the pharaohs, although I am not tempted to worship their pantheon of gods. Christ can speak to me through Saint Shinran Shunin as I walk my dog to and from the park. Obviously I do not see Saint Shinran as a Buddhist would see him. I see him from my point of view as a Christian torn by the horror of man's inhumanity to man. I see him as Christ would have me see him, and with a hope that with Christ's love our swords can be beaten into ploughshares, our bombs defused as we seek food for our overcrowded and hungry planet.

Christ can speak to me through the white china Buddha who sits on my desk at Crosswicks and smiles at me tolerantly when I fly into a torrent of outrage or self-pity. That forbearing smile helps restore my sense of proportion, and rids me of that self-will which keeps me caught up in myself so that I am isolating myself from Christ. Of course I am no more likely to become a Buddhist than my parents were likely to turn to Islam when they framed those lovely verses from the Koran.

There is no limit to the ways in which Christ can speak to us, though for the Christian he speaks first and most clearly through Jesus of Nazareth. Indeed, my icons would be idols if they did not lead me to follow more closely in Jesus' steps.

And Christ spoke to me as I walked through a great column of stone lions leading into the temple at Karnak. We were there at dawn, to avoid flies, tourists, the heat of the sun, and those great soaring columns provoked in us a cathedral sense of awe.

"Why are there so many rams, in the carvings and the frescoes?" someone asked our guide.

To my delight she told us that the ram in the Egyptian temples is Abraham's ram. I remembered that Abraham had indeed been to Egypt, and so had Isaac, and so had Jacob. The desert we were seeing was very much like the desert they had crossed. Because the pharaohs of Abraham's day knew the story of the near-sacrifice of Isaac, and the last-minute substitution of the ram, the Egyptians adopted the ram into their pantheon of gods as a symbol of life.

Possibly Abraham had stood where we were standing; possibly he had even seen the reproductions of the ram, his ram, who had saved Isaac, and thereby Jacob as well.

"Why are there so many cobras?" we asked, "so many vultures and crocodiles?"

"In those days they worshipped what they feared," our guide told us. Placating the gods, it has been called, and it's still something we tend to do if we're not careful. If we view God as a vengeful judge, and turn to Jesus to save us from the furious father, aren't we worshipping what we fear?

Those old Egyptians also worshipped the baboon because every morning when the sun rose, the baboons all clapped their hands for joy, applauding the reappearance of the sun. What a lovely picture, the baboons all clapping their hands and shouting for joy as the sun rose! So it seemed to the Egyptians that the baboons must have had something to do with the rising of the sun, and that their applause helped to bring the sun back up into the sky.

The scarab beetle, too, was an object of worship, because it disappeared down into the desert sands at sundown, and then came up again in the morning as the sun rose, and was, therefore, a symbol of the resurrection for them.

What? The resurrection? Yes, our guide told us, that is what it was called, their firm belief in the resurrection of their bodies, not immediately after their death, but at some unknown future date, which was why so much elaborate preparation went into embalming. I'm not sure how much essential difference there is between the tombs with food and jewels in them, and our own recently abandoned belief that our bones will rise up out of our graves at the Second Coming. Cremation is impermissible because God can't do anything with ashes; if someone dies in a shipwreck and the body is lost at sea and eaten by fish, that's just too bad. Or, if someone is trapped in a burning building and incinerated by fire, that, too, is just too bad. If there is no actual body to be raised, there can be no resurrection. What kind of powerless God is being worshipped? God, who made our bodies, can raise them again from nothing, if need be.

All I know is that neither death, nor life, nor angels, nor principalities, nor powers, nor things present, nor things to come, nor height, nor depth, nor any other creature, shall be able to separate us from the love of God.

And if that is what the ancient Egyptian believed, then we are, at least, cousins.

Hugh and I were in Egypt at the time of the sugar cane cutting. It is harvested today as it was thousands of years ago, cut by hand, with the great sheaves of green loaded onto donkeys' and camels' backs. Time intersected for us as we watched the people working, saw the lush green of land near the Nile, with the Sahara encroaching. Where there was no water, no irrigation, there was sand.

We saw the statue of Rameses II, made famous in Shelley's poem, "Ozymandias." The enormous statue lay in pieces on the sand, and we recited Shelley's lines: *My name is Ozymandias, king of kings. / Look on my works, ye mighty, and despair.*

Our guide was of Islam, and her loving religion was impressive and, rather than making me feel estranged from her, made me feel very close. She was on fire with love of her country and its history, and surely she gave us the equivalent of an advanced college seminar as we moved from temple to temple, archeological site to archeological sight. It was hard not to let our minds become a jumble of gods and pharaohs and warriors and priests and animals and the crowns of upper and lower Egypt.

What we saw told us more about ancient Egypt than it did about the eternal God, as all civilizations reveal more of themselves in their religious practices than they reveal of God. And I began to wonder what we reveal of ourselves as we struggle toward love and understanding of our Maker. What will be said of us in a thousand years if historians study our troubled civilization? What will they write about our forms of worship as they collect artifacts from our churches and cathedrals and temples? Will they understand that for us God is a God of love?

If the ancient Egyptians worshipped what they feared (as well as the celebrating baboons clapping their hands), we worship the God we love and trust. Or do we? Do we show that in our lives? In our care for and concern of each other? If we assume that anybody is outside the Maker's loving concern, aren't we revealing more about ourselves than about God?

There is probably much that we do not understand, or that we misinterpret, as we think of the Egyptians with their rams and scarabs and crocodiles. A friend of mine in the Middle East heard someone say in horror, "Oh, the Christians are the people who drink blood." What a terrible misunderstanding. Perhaps many times we equally fail to understand other peoples and their beliefs.

For the ancient Egyptian there was love and trust in their faith as well as fear. The pharaohs were often referred to as "shepherds," and the god, Osiris, was said to be the shepherd of the underworld. A pyramid text reads, "Thou hast taken them up in thine arms as a shepherd his flock."

The shepherd imagery was particulary vivid to us because we were in Egypt at the time of the new lambs, the baby kids, the foals, the colts. The land was radiant with spring. We saw ancient water wheels being turned by water buffaloes, heads heavy with their curving horns. We saw the people working the land wearing their galabiyehs, those loose-flowing and practical garments which have been worn by working Egyptians for centuries. They are loose and comfortable in the heat; they give protection against flies, and against the sun.

"Thou hast taken them up in thine arms as a shepherd his flock." Did that lovely image pre- or post-date the 23rd Psalm? Was it not a prefiguring of our own Good Shepherd? For me it was beyond contradiction because Christ was, before anything began, always is, and always will be.

I saw a young woman wearing a red sweat shirt patterned with dozens of small white sheep, and *one* black sheep, and I thought of Jesus, the good shepherd, leaving the ninety-nine white sheep and going after the one strayed black sheep, searching until he found the black sheep and put it across his shoulders and carried it home. And he said that there will be more rejoicing over the one repentant sinner than over all the virtuous people who have not strayed. I pray that I, too, will rejoice in the return of the black sheep, and not be like the elder brother in the parable of the Prodigal Son, who really didn't want the father to forgive the repentant black sheep, much less give a party for him.

It is a human tendency to get caught in the self-righteousness of the elder brother, so that we don't want the shepherd to go after the strayed sheep, but to stay in the pen with the virtuous flock. And that is just not scriptural. It is, of course, the forensic stumbling block. If we are forensic, do we then become black sheep ourselves?

In the ancient temples, we saw faces and legs of Egyptian gods scratched out by the early Christians as they took refuge there. Despite their acceptance of Christ as their Lord, we were told, they still believed in the old magic, and the face and feet were supposed to have the most power, so these early Christians took sharp stones and mutilated the paintings and carvings.

Later, in the Coptic museum in Cairo, we saw stone carvings made by the early Christians which had been similarly mutilated by the Muslims.

What are we human beings telling the future about ourselves in what we proclaim about God? Are we saying something loving and creative, or are we being arrogant and spreading fear and suspicion? Are we furthering the coming of the Kingdom, or are we setting up barriers and road blocks?

As I read the papers, listen to the news, I am concerned about what we are telling the future about ourselves, as Christians fight Muslims in Lebanon, as Protestants fight Catholics in Ireland, as acts of terrorism are performed in the name of religion. What are the Right-to-Lifers telling about themselves as they heave bombs into abortion clinics? What are women telling as they proclaim absolute rights to their own bodies?

The Quakers have a way of meeting, without contempt, those with whom they disagree, or those who threaten them. There's a story of a Quaker who heard noises in his house one night, and went downstairs to find a burglar busily stashing things into a pillow case. The Quaker said, "Friend, I would do thee no harm for the world and all that is in it, but thou standest where I am about to shoot." The burglar left.

And yet, there are Protestant and Catholic women who cross battle lines in Ireland to pray with each other. I wonder if that will happen in Lebanon—Christian and Muslim women praying together for peace. White and black women praying together in South Africa? It's not impossible. To cross battle lines to pray is a dimension of the cross which women have long understood. And perhaps it is a special symbol of the cross to *cross* battle lines?

For the human being the cross is an ancient symbol, used thousands of years before Jesus of Nazareth was crucified. The Bushmen of South Africa painted small red crosses in their caves, and it is thought that these small, apricot-skinned people originally came to South Africa from Egypt. They listened for guidance from God in the tapping of the stars. Sometimes on a cold, clear night I think I can hear their tapping, too. The Bushmen were not separated from the stars, or the coinherence of all of creation. Other peoples have tried to exterminate these tiny, untamed people. Surely their loss is felt in great waves throughout the galaxies, an agonizing butterfly effect.

Jesus of Nazareth could not be tamed, either, and so he, too, had to be wiped out, hung on a cross in the dust and the heat and the flies. Those who cannot be tamed are disturbers of the universe, and without them we would be infinitely poorer. But because they are a threat to the control of local governments they must be put down, ruthlessly.

The true universe disturber has no arrogance. The arrogance and vanity of the terrorist is chilling. It takes humility and faith in God's loving concern to cross battle lines, be they geographical or ideological.

I was given a small Mexican cross, a copy of an ancient one, many thousands of years old, and it, like the cross of the African

Bushman, gives me a feeling of continuity and hope. The second person of the Trinity was with us "before the worlds began to be. He is alpha and omega, he the source, the ending," as the ancient hymn says. All of God has always been part of creation, part of the story, taking us in the everlasting arms as the shepherd clasps the lost lamb.

I don't want a closed-in religion of smug sheep, a religion in which all the answers are given and honest questions are discouraged. I don't want a religion which allows me to feel superior, or which gives me the truth denied to others.

So what am I looking for? What is my hope?

First, I must accept that I am broken, as all we human beings are broken, but that my creative urge toward healing and health is strong, and that I can be healed with the blood of the Lamb (how lovely that Christ is both shepherd and lamb!). I want to be willing to do God's will, but not to superimpose my will on el's. The distinction is not always easy. I want to help the battered bride to become beautiful. I want to be ready to meet the bridegroom, and so be part of the heavenly kingdom and the redemption of all things.

Sometimes something small and unexpected will turn on a brilliant light for me. Every other summer for the past several years I have taught a writers' workshop at Mundelein College. Many of the people who are taking this two-week course for credit are teachers, going on for their Masters degrees, or their Ph.D.s. One afternoon in the large room overlooking Lake Michigan, where we sat in a circle, we spent an hour sharing stories which meant something to us. One of these stories was that of the old man by the river who did not recognize what God sent him. A few of the stories brought healing tears. And one, for me, brought glory:

A teacher of small children told us of a child who said to her, "Jesus is God's show and tell."

How simple and how wonderful! Jesus is God's show and

tell. That's the best theology of incarnation I've ever heard. Jesus said, if you do not understand me as a little child, you will not be able to enter the kingdom of heaven.

That child's insight works more powerfully for me than dogma. When I am informed that Jesus of Nazareth was exactly like us except sinless, I block. If he was sinless he wasn't exactly like us. That makes no sense. Jesus was like us because he was born like any human child, grew up like the rest of us, asked questions in the temple when he was twelve, lost his temper in righteous indignation at the money lenders in the temple, grieved when at the end his disciples abandoned him. I want Jesus to be like us because he is God's show and tell, and too much dogma obscures rather than reveals the likeness.

If Jesus is God's show and tell, the wonder, the marvel is that Jesus and the Father are one. Not I, says Jesus over and over, but the Father in me, the Father who is such love that he is willing to be in the story with us.

Alleluia.

But God's show and tell includes the cross. For us all.

Many years ago when our children were small, I encountered my first Episcopal monk, a priest of the Order of the Holy Cross. Although I am what is called "a cradle Episcopalian," I hadn't known that there were Episcopal monks or nuns. This was a gentle young man who had just come back to this country after several years in Liberia, and who had been brought to Crosswicks for tea by a mutual friend. He said, "Don't be afraid to make the sign of the cross. All it means is: God be in my thoughts, and in my heart, and in my left hand, and in my right hand, all through this day and night." That was another illumination for me. It helps me to ask God to be in me, to be in my head and my heart and my left hand and my right hand. That may tell more about me than about God, but I am not ashamed to admit that I need God in me, in all of me, in my down-sitting and in my up-rising.

While I was in bed last summer, bleeding, hurting, a friend sent me a tape of a record of Hildegarde of Bingen, *A Feather on the Breath of God*. Hildegarde, a medieval abbess, was on fire with her passionate love of God, and she was not afraid to use passionate language to express her love. Listening to the singing on the tape was another part of my healing. Hildegarde's love of the Creator and of creation reminded me of Ikhnaton, the only pharaoh we know about who worshipped one God with adoring love, Aton, the sun, the giver of life. Ikhnaton's hymns to Aton would have been understood by Hildegarde. Perhaps they sometimes sing together now.

The sun is feared as well as revered in desert countries, where the fierce rays of the heat of the day burn and parch, and only the annual flooding of the Nile keeps Egypt's shores green. Ikhnaton wrote love poems to his one God which, as our guide recited them, reminded me of John of the Cross as well as Hildegarde of Bingen. During this young pharaoh's brief reign he rejected polytheism, forbidding the worship of many gods, and turned all the passion of his adoration to Aton. This inevitably shook the domain of the powerful priests and they had to get rid of him. They murdered him.

He had some kind of glandular imbalance which deformed his lower body, swelling his abdomen so that he was pear-shaped. But unlike other pharaohs he allowed sculptures to be made of himself as he actually was, rather than demanding the usual glorified image—what the pharaohs wanted people to think they were like.

I was awed by Ikhnaton's bravery in overriding the extremely powerful and ruthless priests of the old gods, and proclaiming the one God. I was awed also by his acceptance of himself exactly as he was, without one plea. Our guide, too, felt drawn to him, saying that he was somewhat like Sadat, defying danger in order to remain true to what he believed—and that was the greatest compliment she could have given him.

I knew, as I stood looking at the statue of Ikhnaton, at his sensitive, intelligent face, that there is nothing he could say, nothing Hildegarde of Bingen, or John of the Cross, or Lancelot Andrewes, or any single one of us can say about God which is adequate. What we say about God may explain us, our warm or cold-heartedness, our humility or our vanity, our loving forgiveness or our resentful demands for vindication. But it cannot explain God.

Probably the Egyptian priests thought they were correct in killing Ikhnaton, just as the high priest thought he was doing the right thing in condemning Jesus to crucifixion. To wipe out anyone from God's love is a form of murder, even if it is not literally acted out. One way or another, most of us commit some form of murder every day, and we need to repent, and ask for forgiveness, so that we may turn to love in a world which is anything but fair.

Then I thought of the parable of the workers in the vineyard, and how we really don't think it's fair for the owner of the vineyard to give the man who worked only the last hour the same wages as those who worked all through the heat of the day. After all, it's not *fair!* But when we insist on that kind of fairness, aren't we thinking forensically? This kind of thinking inevitably leads to a forensic view of Jesus and the cross—a view which may be long on justice, but is short on love.

If we receive nothing but justice, untempered by mercy, not one of us will be invited to the heavenly banquet, not even those who teach that the banquet is prepared only for the selected few.

It won't do. What about all those ancient Egyptians with their longing for resurrection? What about Ikhnaton and his love of the one God? Can there never be a party for them? Will not God bring out the silken robes and order the fatted calf to be prepared? What about those who worshipped what they feared—the vulture, the cobra, the crocodile? And the baboons, clapping their hands for joy at the rising of the sun?

Will all those born before Christ be excluded from the party? Didn't God make them, too? I don't have any answers here, just a lot of questions and hopes, about a God of love who prefers parties to punishments.

I don't understand why the idea of emptying hell upsets some people so. To be upset about it is to think forensically, and while we all suffer from a touch of this, we can surely recognize our own lack of generosity. If we don't, how can we enjoy the party any more than did the prodigal son's elder brother? Do we, too, want to go out and sulk?

I don't need to know how God is going to make it all come out all right in the end, but it is God, not us creatures, who will see to the coming of the Kingdom, and el is not going to fail with Creation, not with me, not with any of us.

God be in my thoughts, and in my heart. In my left hand and in my right hand. Atone me. At-one me with you and your love. Help me to pray for those I fear as well as those I love, knowing that you can take my most ungracious prayers and give them grace. Whenever we pray, we are tapping the power of creation, and that's a mighty power. There are a lot of battle lines to cross in order for us to pray with each other, and with the rest of the world, with those who do not agree with us, with those who worship God in ways we do not understand. But that is all right. We do not have to understand. We do have to try to turn to love, to know that the Lord who created all, also loves all that which was made.

It is easy for me to pray for the Egyptologist who taught me so much. She loves God, and so we have that in common. That is enough.

It is far less easy for me to pray for the terrorists, or even for those two men who sat in the courtroom last January and wished the jurors no good. It is not easy for me to pray for the forces of evil in this world expressing themselves through their lust for power, their greed, their corruption in high places. But if I take the cross seriously, that is part of the demand. These are people for whom Jesus died.

At this point I'm not sure I want those two men who stared so malevolently at us poor jurors to come to the party, but it won't be complete until they are there, come to themselves, turned, returned to love, part of the at-one-ment.

Somehow I am helped when I remember the baboons clapping their hands and calling for joy that the sun is coming up again over the horizon, that night is over, and the Light of the world is bright.

Redeeming the Symbols

11

DURING THE YEARS WHEN WE WERE raising our children and living in Crosswicks year 'round, being part of the community of the Congregational Church in the center of the village, there were no symbols of any kind in the church. Today there is a plain wooden cross. A quarter of a century ago that was taboo. When the minister said, "let us pray," we did no more than slightly bow our heads: any more would have been capitulating to Rome. When I directed the choir in a Latin anthem, we half expected the roof to collapse on our heads. Following the calendar of the church year was unheard of. The word *liturgy* was not in our vocabulary.

I knew true Christian community in that church, but I missed symbols. As a story-teller I live by symbol. It fills and feeds me so that in a symbol-less church I feel undernourished. It is true that any symbol can be made into an idol. Any symbol can be elevated or distorted into something it was not meant to be. But that does not destroy the truth of the original symbol.

Was God not showing Jacob a marvellous symbol in the glorious ladder of angels?

A few Christmasses ago my son and daughter-in-law gave me a pretty pair of silver earrings. Each earring was in the shape of a crescent moon, containing a scattering of stars. I don't think any of us realized that this was the Proctor and Gamble logo until the recent brouhaha in which it was alleged that this logo was an ancient trade mark of the devil. So much noise has been made about this that sales have fallen, and I understand that this logo is to be phased out, and no longer used on Proctor and Gamble products.

What!?! The crescent moon and the stars Satan's symbol? How can that possibly be? Who *made* the moon and the stars? Genesis makes it very clear that the heavens are the Lord's, and that el is the loving Creator of the universe. How can we be so stupid as to call the loveliness of the night sky a sign of Satan? I am totally baffled.

And horrified. I am not about to give over the beauty of moon and stars to Satan or to Satan worshippers. God took Abraham out at night to see the stars, the stars made in the mighty acts of creation. The Maker's stars. The Maker's moon.

In some early civilizations the crescent moon was a symbol of worship of the goddess, Ishtar or Ashtaroth, and other female deities, like Diana, whose symbol was the moon. These goddesses were said to be benificent when the moon was waxing, and maleficent when it was waning. In countries where the crops followed the phases of the moon, where earth was mother, the worship of the moon goddess was natural. In the western world of Protestantism we have swung to the opposite extreme, criticizing the Roman Catholics for their reverence of Mary, the most holy birth-giver (as the orthodox call her), and have emphasized a masculine, patriarchal God who sometimes seems to have more of the attributes of Zeus with his bolts of lightning, than the loving Abba of Jesus.

Perhaps the fear of the symbol of the crescent moon and the stars is a masculine fear of the feminine. But we need to regain the feminine, the intuitive, the nurturing element in ourselves, and in our understanding of the Godhead, our Maker, who is all in all, mother, father, brother, sister, lover, friend, companion. The great mystics of the church, such as Hildegarde of Bingen, Meister Eckhardt, Lady Julian of Norwich, were casual about the gender of God, using the male or female pronoun as the need arose. Let us not be bullied into fearing the feminine symbol of the crescent moon. We see our tides swing to the rhythm of the moon. Our bodies follow the moon's phases. Our words *month* and *Monday* come from the same source. Our dependence on the rhythm of the moon is part of the interdependence of all nature, all life, all Creation.

Christ's cross has been a vital symbol throughout the ages; it does not belong exclusively to the Christian era. The butterfly (like the ram) has long been a symbol of metamorphosis and resurrection, adding new meaning to the "butterfly effect."

The extraordinary world of particle physics is providing new symbols for me, and new understanding of old symbols. My response to my discovery of Einstein's theories of relativity and Planck's quantum theory was to write *A Wrinkle in Time*, as I struggled to understand the wonders of the Creator and creation.

Was it a coincidence that I picked up Berdyaev's book warning against a forensic view of God just as I started jury duty and especially just as I needed to pay heed to this message? Or that I began to read about particle physics with its theory of the total interdependence of all creation just when the church and the world seemed to be shattering into inimical, isolated fragments? Is there such a thing as coincidence? (A priest friend told me that "a coincidence is a small miracle in which God prefers to remain anonymous.")

So it did not surprise me when I settled myself in my seat for a plane journey, that I opened the New York Times science section to an article on particle physics; nor that the two books I carried in my bag were Robert Alter's *The Art of Biblical Narrative,* and John Boslough's *Stephen Hawking's Universe,* and that all three were mutually nourishing, each reinforcing the others.

The world of particle physics is a new world in my generation, and has revealed a universe of such complexity that even the greatest physicists do not fully comprehend it.

My parents, growing to adulthood in those strangely placid years before World War I, lived in a far simpler world. Their understanding of the nature of the universe was closer to that of Jacob's day than of ours, so rapidly has our knowledge grown. For them, despite the fact that it was acknowledged that stars are suns, and our planet part of an ordinary solar system, creation was infinitely smaller and easier to comprehend than it is today. Ants and gnats and the no-seeum-bugs that came out in the spring were as small as anyone needed to comprehend. There were smaller things, such as germs and viruses, which could be seen only through microscopes, but, still, they could be *seen.*

And then the heart of the atom was opened. Scientists, struggling to make a bomb to end all bombs, were given more money for their research than ever they would have been given in time of peace. How did they dare set off that first atom bomb, when they were not at all sure that it would not start a chain reaction that would blow up the entire planet? And yet, knowing of this possibility, they went ahead. Was it bravery or folly?

Whichever it was it has opened up a new understanding of the universe, and it is up to us to try to understand it creatively, as a further revelation of the wonders of the mind of the Maker.

I turn to the study of astrophysics and particle physics because these disciplines are about the nature of being, and so may be for us revelations of what God is like, and how Christ's love works to enflame our own.

So I sat on the plane, fastened my seat belt, and started the Times article, by Walter Sullivan, and read that not only do quanta (subatomic particles) have the ability to communicate instantaneously, but according to French theorist Bernard d'Espagnat, such instantaneous signals exceed the speed of light.

What does that mean, I wondered? And then I remembered that we have instances of inexplicable, instantaneous communication in our own lives. There are stories, many authenticated, of people calling each other, instantaneously, across vast distances. A mother will sit up in bed, abruptly wakened from sleep, and rush, unthinking to make a phone call. Her moment of waking comes just as the grandbaby begins to choke, and the call alerts the parents and the baby is reached just in time.

My grandfather had passage on the Titanic; his bags had already gone onto the ship, when a voice told him to leave the gang plank, not to sail. The warning was so clear that he heeded it.

We don't understand such phenomena any more than physicists understand the behaviour of some sub-atomic particles. But this is no reason to say that such things do not happen. It is no reason to say they are works of the Devil, rather than of Christ. There are many occurrences that we must admit we do not understand. As long as this world belongs to the Word who made all that was made, that is all we need to know. Maybe one day, as we develop spiritually, we will understand more than we do now. When we are in heaven, in the Presence, we will "know as we are known."

Quantum mechanics, according to the Times article, "indicates that properties usually attributed to matter have no real existence until measured."

This parallels Parker Palmer's affirmation that the self becomes real only when reacting with other selves. We do not become real in isolation, but in response to the others we encounter along the way, and who call us into being, as the observing scientist calls quanta into being.

And how do we, ourselves, become real? Hugh married an introverted, shy, undefined young woman. I became real as I responded to him, to our children, to our friends, who quite literally *brought me out* of the shell in which I had hidden myself.

Destructive criticism is devastating because it does not make *real;* instead, it negates and destroys. Constructive criticism builds, bringing out the hidden reality.

In the world of particle physics, I am encountering a new reality, which enlarges and enhances my own.

The indeterminacy of quantum mechanics seems to upset scientists as much as it does theologians. But why is this "probability" aspect of quantum mechanics more perplexing than the "probability" aspect of sperm?

Of all the thousands of the male sperm ejected during coitus, only one will meet and unite with the female ovum. Which one? Who can guess? Is it complete indeterminacy? Had another sperm met and united with my egg, I would have a very different child from the one who came from the particular sperm and ovum which succeeded in bonding.

Yet this randomness in the mechanism of human reproduction doesn't seem to upset anybody, and it has been known, at least since biblical times, that the male sperm, as well as the female egg, is needed for conception.

Just after I wrote these thoughts in my journal, I picked up Alter's book and read about "the vigorous movement of biblical writing away from the stable closure of the mythological world, and toward the *indeterminacy,* the shifting causal concatenations, the ambiguity of a fiction made to resemble the uncertainties of life in history." Fascinating to come across the word *indeterminacy* in two such different contexts, though I don't agree with Alter's definition of "the mythological world" as offering "stable closure." It's the old misuse of the word *mythological,* and I might rather substitute the word, "cultic." The important thing is that both the world of Scripture and the world of quantum mechanics are worlds of indeterminacy. That is a freeing thought, because a world of determinacy is a world where everything is preordained beforehand, where there is no free will.

I shudder at the once widely-accepted theory that God preordained us all before we were born for either heaven or hell, and nothing we did would change this predestination. What kind of god would predestine part of his creation to eternal damnation? This is surely not consistent with God's creation in the early chapters of Genesis, when Elohim looked at all that had been made and called it good, very good. And yet this brutal theology used to be widely accepted and taught, a kind of spiritual terrorism.

One time when I was visiting my family in Lincoln, England, I was given a tour of the cathedral. Two things remain with me. We went into the cathedral through one of the side doors, and a wooden inset in the stone arch above the door was pointed out. This had been put into the arch to hold a canopy so that a king could walk under it, protected from the elements. Since that time, nobody had bothered to take down the inset. The king was Richard the Second.

Suddenly I realized how very old England is. Crosswicks, well over two hundred years old, seems ancient in North America, but many places in England and on the European continent are so much older that our oldest buildings seem new in comparison.

The other thing that has stayed firmly in my mind is a story. After we had been through the cathedral, we went to the library, one of the most beautiful buildings I have ever seen, with an unusually fine collection of books. The dean who went into exile at the time of Cromwell spent his years away from England in Holland, which was then the center of the book world. He returned with a superb collection of books.

On one of the walls of his library hangs the portrait of a

woman with a pleasant face, and a ruff around her neck. This was the dean's mother. Long before he was born, this woman, then a young girl, was convinced that she was one of those predestined to be damned. This was her firm conviction, and it did not make her very merry. One evening she was having dinner with some friends, and they tried to assure her that she could not be certain that she was damned. But, she told them, she was certain, absolutely certain. "I am as certain that I am damned as that this wine glass will shatter when I fling it to the stone floor." She flung down the fragile glass. It did not shatter.

So she cheered up, married, and ultimately became the mother of the dean.

Thank God for indeterminacy!

There are people, however, who seem so plagued by terrible things that it would indeed seem that they have been damned. In their lives one tragedy follows another. It is a terrible mystery. But do not come to me when something terrible has happened saying, "It's God's will." No! Death, disease, murder, may be from man's error, but never God's will. In the face of suffering and tragedy, we can only have faith that somehow, ultimately, in God's time all wounds will be healed.

For God is the God of love, and love will not rest while there is any suffering left, any rebellion, any anguish. The song of the stars in their courses will not return to the full beauty of the ancient harmonies until the coming again in glory of the Lord of Love.

* ✳ *

The great British biophysicist, J.B.S. Haldane, said that "The universe is not only stranger than we imagine, it's stranger than anything we can imagine."

More recently, Douglas Adams, in introducing Chapter One of *The Restaurant at the End of the Universe,* wrote, "There is a theory which states that if ever anyone discovers exactly what the Universe is for, and why it is here, it will instantly disappear and be replaced by something even more bizarre and inexplicable. There is another which states that this has already happened."

I laugh, and yet I marvel, too. If the universe is in a state of flux (one theory), expanding out from a mass denser and smaller than a subatomic particle, to form all the galaxies, moving out into the darkness of space, ever further away and further apart, until the procedure reverses itself and pulls back in until once again it is the infinitely small primal unity, who is to say that God's design is going to be the same every time? And what about the theories of alternate universes, or multiple universes? These concepts are frightening only if we forget that whatever it is, and however it is, it is God's. And as long as the Maker knows what it is all about, and as long as we test our speculations against the Love of God, as well as the laboratory, all shall be well.

Haldane's description of the universe as "stranger than anything we can imagine," is an exciting one for me, because nothing is strange for the Creator of it all. And in the fullness of time, *kairos,* God's time, we, too, shall see the full glory as it really is.

Alter, in *The Art of Biblical Narrative,* refers to the "double dialectic between design and disorder, providence and freedom. The various biblical narratives . . . [form] a spectrum between the opposing extremes of disorder and design." He is talking about the Bible, but he could just as well be talking about particle physics. Or about our own lives, which often seem an incomprehensible mixture of accident and pattern. We are created by God, who has given us free will. Therefore we can work either for or against God's design. It is a splendid paradox.

And, as always with paradox, it can be expressed best in symbols.

I am more at home with the symbols which come from astro- and particle physics than I am with those which are coming from the computer. The computer, it has been suggested, is going to change the way we think, and I hope that we will use enough free will so that this change will be constructive, not disastrous. But great care must be taken.

The computer has proved itself to be anything but infallible. It can make horrendous mistakes, including the near precipitation of nuclear war. Daily it makes minor mistakes, and not long ago I was the victim of one of them.

I had been on an intense and overscheduled lecture tour in the Pacific Northwest. On the last day, when I was in Spokane, Washington, at a Young Writers Conference, I phoned to reconfirm my flight home to New York the next day. I was told that everything was fine, I was in the computer, but my flight would leave at 11:25 A.M., rather than 11:35, as my ticket said. Fine. No problem.

The next day I went to the airport bright and early, ready to relax and sleep on the long flight home. I handed over my ticket, and the man behind the counter looked at it and told me, "That flight was cancelled three weeks ago."

"But I reconfirmed it yesterday!"

He played for a long time with his computer. Finally he looked up, saying, "I think the computer thought you were leaving from Portland, Oregon."

"As you can see," I replied icily, "I am in Spokane, Washington. What are you going to do?"

Again he played with his computer, and at last offered to send me to Chicago's O'Hare Airport where I could change planes and . . .

"No," I said flatly. "Not O'Hare. I am too exhausted for O'Hare."

Finally he sent me to Seattle, where I had to go from one arm of the satellite to another as far away as possible, changing planes and airlines, and accept the fact that I would get to New

York several hours later than I had expected, and at the airport furthest from Manhattan.

I capsized into my seat, telling the sympathetic hostess what had happened. "To err is human," she said. "To foul it up completely takes a computer."

I was so exhausted that I reached for the airline magazine and began leafing through it. Almost immediately I came across an article describing in glowing terms the world of the microchip which we are inheriting. And I read, appalled; "What the automobile has done for the legs, what television has done for the eyes, the computer will do for the mind."

No!

I don't like what the automobile has done for our legs, or what television has done for our eyes, and I certainly do not want the computer to manipulate our minds.

The computer, unlike subatomic particles, or biblical stories, is deterministic. It does not ask questions. It gives answers, sometimes useful ones, sometimes not, as when it "thought" I was leaving from Portland, Oregon.

The computer is either/or. Yes/No. There is no room for *perhaps,* or *on the other hand.* There is no room for complexity which draws us into contradiction and paradox.

The computer is here to stay. I can't afford to put my head in the sand, like the ostrich, and hope it will go away. Ultimately, when word processors become a lot more portable than they are at present, and suit my needs better, I'll likely write with one. I already have a six pound little electronic typestar, which is even more sensitive to my fingers and my mind than the heavy old electric typewriter. But I don't want the computer to change my way of thinking without so much as a by–your–leave.

The indeterminacy of both Bible and physics is symbolically far more creative than the determinacy of high technocracy.

Fritjov Capra, in *The Tao of Physics,* quotes atomic physicist

Robert Oppenheimer: "If we ask, for instance, whether the position of the electron remains the same, we must say 'no;' if we ask whether the electron's position changes with time, we must say 'no;' if we ask whether the electron is at rest, we must say 'no;' if we ask whether the electron is in motion, we must say 'no.'"

He also quotes from the Upanishads:

It moves, it moves not.
It is far, it is near.
It is within all this.
And outside all this.

There appears to be a tacit assumption that the world of particle physics and the world of eastern mysticism (Hinduism, Buddhism) are compatible, but not the worlds of particle physics and Christianity. This is not only blindness on the part of those who claim this, it is a misunderstanding of Christianity. Christianity *is* an Eastern religion. It is to our shame that we have westernized it, imposed on it our forensic thinking. But if we go back to the Gospels and the good news Jesus brought us, the contradictory, paradoxical elements of the new physics fit most compatibly with those of Scripture.

"Before Abraham was, I am," Jesus proclaimed. He spoke with Moses and Abraham on the mountain, overriding chronological time. When Moses asked God, "What is your name?" God replied, "I will be what I will be."

The Athanasian creed surely cannot be understood in terms of Western logic: God the Father incomprehensible. God the Son incomprehensible. God the Holy Spirit incomprehensible . . .

That is surely oriental, rather than occidental thinking, or rather, it is truly cosmic thinking.

Listen to the Lord speaking in Isaiah 55:

For my thoughts are not your thoughts,
  neither are your ways my ways, says the Lord.
For as the heavens are higher than the earth,
  so are my ways higher than your ways
  and my thoughts than your thoughts.
For as the rain and the snow come down from heaven
  and return not thither but water the earth,
making it bring forth and sprout,
  giving seed to the sower and bread to the eater,
so shall my word be that goes forth from my mouth;
  it shall not return to me empty,
but it shall accomplish that which I purpose,
  and prosper in the thing for which I sent it.

Then there is Hildegarde of Bingen likening herself to a feather on the breath of God, and Julian of Norwich seeing the entire universe in "the quantity of a hazelnut." Henry Vaughan "saw eternity the other night like a great ring of pure and endless light."

In an equally "eastern" mode of thinking, the anonymous author of *The Cloud of Unknowing* wrote thus: "Heaven ghostly, as high down as up, and as up as down, behind as before, on one side as another. Insomuch, that whoso had a true desire for to be at heaven, then that same time he were in heaven ghostly. For the high and the next way thither is run by desires and not by paces of feet."

Beyond cold rationalism, such a way of viewing heaven's reality reminds me of the words of St. Paul as he spoke to the people at Corinth:

The foolishness of God is wiser than men . . . God has chosen things that are not, to bring to nothing things that are . . . For we impart a secret and hidden wisdom of God . . . What no eye has seen, no ear heard, nor the heart of man conceived,

God has prepared for those who love him.

This is for me a happy and comprehensible understanding of heaven. It is by accepting all the "contra-dictions," these indeterminate non-answers, that we are given an intuition of heaven. If we do not recognize it now, by "a true desire," it will be all the more difficult later. Heaven is nothing we can seek through our own virtue; it cannot be earned; it is a gift of the God of love. When we are self-emptied enough to make room for this love, it is not as a result of our own moral rectitude or willpower. But it is sometimes given to us, this lovely emptiness, and then the Holy Spirit can fill it, with prayer, or music, or a poem, or a story. Or, sometimes, it goes beyond all these to the greatest gift of all, being filled with that which is beyond all symbols, with God's Presence.

And then we *are,* far more than when we are filled with self-probing, self-centeredness, or self-righteousness.

Gregory of Nyssa expresses this in language which is just as difficult as the language of particle physics, but which is rich indeed:

> Abraham passed through all the reasoning that is possible to human nature about the divine attributes, and after he had purified his mind of all such concepts, he took hold of a faith that was unmixed and pure of any concept, and he fashioned for himself this ikon of knowledge of God that is completely free from error, namely the belief that God completely transcends any knowable symbol.

We are closest to contemplation when we move into, through, and beyond symbol, but during most of our lives we need symbols, such as this of Saint Bonaventura: "God is a circle whose center is everywhere, and whose circumference nowhere."

Numbers are symbols, powerful symbols. Combined with letters of the alphabet, as equations, they can change our way of looking at the universe.

Einstein's most famous equation is $E = MC^2$: Energy equals mass plus the speed of light squared—a symbol so potent that the depths of its implications have not yet been plumbed. And, like all symbols, it can draw us closer to God to whom all numbers belong, or it can be a barrier between us and the Creator.

I had a letter from a young woman who asked me seriously whether or not the number 6 belongs to the Devil. I replied that if everything belongs to the Creator, then so do numbers, and the Devil can't take over a number unless we are willing to give it to him. Where did she get the idea that number 6 belongs to the Devil? From 666?

According to Revelation 13:18, 666 is the number of the beast: "If anyone has insight let him calculate the number of the beast, for it is man's number. His number is 666." The beast is often assumed to be Satan (the sum of the letters in Nero Caesar in Hebrew adds up to 666). But even numbers, when abused, can be redeemed, and ultimately 666 will return to God.

Slowly I have learned the beauty of numbers, particularly as I studied harmony and counterpoint on the piano and learned the intricacies of the fugue. Through music I have come to see numbers as a way of giving glory to God, and I would rather dwell on the bright side, not the dark side, of a symbol.

In Jacob's day, numbers were for counting your camels, your sheep. And the stars were a symbol of numbers beyond the human capacity to count.

Jacob came from a small, insignificant tribe on a sparsely populated planet. Yet he, like his father and grandfather, was told that his descendants would be as the stars of the sky, as the grains of sand. In God's eyes, insignificance doesn't even exist. If something *is,* then it is significant.

Particle physics has a similar sense of the absolute significance of the very small, the so incredibly small we can't even imagine such smallness.

In *Particles,* Michael Chester writes, "Not only does [the neutrino] have zero charge, it has zero mass. The neutrino is a spinning little bit of nothingness that travels at the speed of light."

I love that! A spinning little bit of nothingness! It so delights me that I wrote a Christmas song about it.

> The neutrino and the unicorn
> Danced the night that Christ was born.
> A spinning little bit of nothingness
> that travels at the speed of light
> an unseen spark of somethingness
> is all that can hold back the night.
> The tiny neutron splits in two,
> an electron and a proton form.
> Where is the energy that is lost?
> Who can hold back the impending storm?
> Cosmic collapse would be the cost.
> A spinning nothing, pure and new,
> The neutrino comes to heal and bless.
> The neutrino and the unicorn
> danced the night that Christ was born.
> The sun is dim, the stars are few,
> The earthquake comes to split and shake.
> All purity of heart is lost,
> In the black density of night
> stars fall. O will the heavens break?
> Then through the tingling of black frost
> the unicorn in silver dress
> crosses the desert, horn alight.
> Earth's plates relax their grinding stress.

The unicorn comes dancing to
make pure again, redeem and bless,
 The neutrino and the unicorn
 danced the night that Christ was born.

Pauli postulated the existence of the neutrino to account for the tiny amount of energy lost when a neutron breaks into a proton and an electron. Energy can*not* be lost—and the neutrino, thus far, is the best explanation: a spinning little bit of nothingness that travels at the speed of light.

We human beings do like explanations, and we'd really prefer them to be simple, if not simplistic. But the postulation of the neutrino is as wildly imaginative as those angels ascending and descending the ladder joining heaven and earth. And each postulation that seems to be a workable one leads on to even wilder uses of the imagination—not the imagination gone insane (though we must accept that possibility), but the imagination exploring all probabilities and possibilities.

If the neutrino is, it is God's, and it is as valued by el as Jacob. Or you. Or me.

The concept of subatomic particles plays havoc with ordinary concepts of time. Chester writes:

> Actually, one millionth of a second is not so brief on a subatomic time scale. Both the pion with its lifetime of one-hundred millionth of a second and the muon with one millionth of a second are extremely long-lasting. Compare these times with the time that it takes a pion to interact with a nucleon, and they are enormous time-spans. Comparing the pion-nucleon interaction to the pion lifetime is like comparing one second to 100 million years. Comparing the pion-nucleon interaction to the muon lifetime is like comparing one second to ten billion years.

Is that any more formidable to think about than comparing the lifetime of a human being to the lifetime of a sun, or to the lifetime of a galaxy?

It makes sense only if we think of it all as part of our rootedness in cosmos, our *enkosmismene*. And it knocks our ordinary concepts of chronological time into a cocked hat. Time, as chronology, makes me dizzy with both lack of meaning and unreachable meaning. We need ordinary, chronological time so that we can, for instance, get to the airport or to the office on time, but here time is only an agreed upon fiction so that we will be enabled to get through the day's work with as little confusion as possible. And even in flying across the continent, our bodies are agonizingly jolted with time change and jet lag, so that we become aware that our bodies do function in ordinary time.

Yet, when I think of the pion and the muon, of the great spiral galaxies, and of our own little lives in terms of *kairos*—of rootedness in cosmos, in God's time itself—it opens vast vistas which can be awesome, even terrifying ("What a dreadful place is this!" Jacob cries), but less terrifying than it is wondrous, because God's time is far more real than ordinary *chronos*, and we are part of both.

During our mortal lives, however, *chronos* is not merely illusion. My body is aging according to human chronology, not nucleon or galactic chronology. My knees creak. My vision is variable. My energy span is shorter than I think it ought to be. There is nothing I can do to stop the passage of this kind of time in which we human beings are set. I can work with it rather than against it, but I cannot stop it. I do not like what it is doing to my body. If I live as long as many of my forbears, these outward diminishments will get worse, not better. But these are the outward signs of chronology, and there is another Madeleine who is untouched by them, the part of me that lives forever in *kairos* and bears God's image.

(My mother said, "I may be an old woman in my eighties, but inside me I am still a dancing girl.")

In particle physics there is a theory, posited by Feynman, that positrons are electrons travelling backwards in time. The positron, unlike the human creature, is not bound by one-way linear time—the past-to-future track—but can move backwards in time as well as forwards. That's fine for the positron, but not for the human being. Who wants second childhood in an old body?

To move backwards as well as forwards is still linear. *Kairos* is not bound by time at all. And that marvel which makes us unique as well as inter-dependent is free in *kairos*.

As I type these words I am in Crosswicks, where Hugh and I are house- and animal-sitting while Bion and Laurie are away. The mercury is sub-zero, and the anti-freeze in one of the pipes leading to the tower—my over-the-garage study—has frozen, and the tower is a deep freeze, and unusable until the mercury climbs to thirty, and the anti-freeze thaws, and we find where the problem is.

Anti-freeze shouldn't freeze! I am sitting in the corner of the kitchen-dining room where my son has his desk, and through the windows I look past the three tall spruce trees to the sun slanting against the bare branches of a maple and outlining them in gold. The ground is white, and the hills beyond the fields are mauve. These hills are old, many thousands of years old, worn down through the years by wind and rain. The spruce trees, now more than thirty feet high, were given me as a mother's day present more than three decades ago; the dark smudges of the brussels sprouts plants, the only vegetables left in the garden, were planted last June; the snow fell only a few days ago. In that one glance I have seen a considerable spread of chronology. This is something I might not have noticed before my fascination with particle physics. I read Michael Chester's book this past summer, often while in the waiting room at the hospital lab between various tests while we were trying to get rid of the aeromonas.

Particle physicists talk about "strange particles," seemingly less afraid of that which is strange than are many people looking for a safe religion. Was it because Isaac's God was strange and anything but "safe" that Jacob was so slow in taking El Shaddai as his God?

Chester says, "There was a serious problem concerning these new particles. They were all [kaons] created in strong interactions, but decayed slowly to weak interactions. This was very unexpected. Physicists were used to the idea that particle events are essentially reversible. A particle born in the instant of operation of the strong force should not fade away over the vast ages of time (such as one billionth of a second or even one millionth of a second) required by a weak force. Because of this peculiar imbalance, these new particles were given the name of *strange particles.*" (Scientists can be as upset by the unexpected in the universe as theologians.)

Chester goes on to say, "Certainly the physical universe is much more dreamlike and much less mechanical than we generally realize."

The physicist can and sometimes does say that the physical universe exists only in the mind.

Whose mind? The mind of the physicist with an imagination as wild as that of the teller of fairy tales? Haldane says we cannot imagine it. Whose mind, then? The mind of God?

With our capacity to misuse, abuse, or even annihilate our planet with all we have learned about the physical universe, what are we doing to the glorious designs of the mind of God? It is one of the problems and responsibilities of free will, and, unless we believe in predestination, in a deterministic universe, we can't let ourselves off the hook of personal responsibility. Though the butterfly may not be aware that it affects galaxies thousands of light years away, we humans are given at least an inkling of the results of our most casual actions.

A small example is cigarette smoking. If I am in a room where someone is smoking, not only does it irritate my eyes, but I am being made a passive smoker, like it or not, and receiving all the detrimental effects of the cigarette as much as if I were smoking it. We can do nothing in isolation, no matter how much we try to separate ourselves from our cosmic community.

* ✳ *

A true symbol is an open window, never leading to a closed, deterministic world, but to an open, indeterministic one. Symbols are mind, heart, and soul stretchers.

Recently I was shown a colour photograph of an icon—from Armenia, I think—which absolutely delights me. It is a picture of King David, sitting and holding his harp with one hand. With the other he holds a child who is sitting on his knee, and the caption under the picture reads: *King David with Christ on his lap.*

What a glorious reminder that Christ always was! Jesus of Nazareth lived for a brief life span, but Christ always was, is, and will be, and the picture of King David with Christ on his lap is my treasure for this year, a treasure largely in my mind's eye, because I do not have a copy of the picture of this icon.

So, like King David, we may hold Christ on our laps, and we will be taught to live lovingly with paradox and contradiction, with yes and with no, light and dark, in and out, up and down.

Jacob, wrestling with the angel, was in his own way holding on to Christ. And the angel blessed him.

After that glory he went on and tried to bribe Esau to forgive him, typical Jacob-fashion. And Esau "ran to meet him, and embraced him, and fell on his neck, and kissed him, and they wept."

Esau wept with joy to see his brother again. And Jacob?

Were they tears of relief that Esau wasn't still angry?

Esau did not want all the gifts Jacob had brought in order to placate him. He said, "I have enough, my brother. Keep what is yours."

But Jacob urged him, "Take, I pray you, my blessing that is brought to you, because God has dealt graciously with me." And he urged him, and he took it.

The King James translation uses the word *blessing.* Jacob has just been blessed by the angel who wrestled with him all night and smote him on the thigh. He also has his father, Isaac's, blessing, stolen from Esau. Surely it is time for him to give a blessing to his brother.

The Jerusalem Bible uses the word *gift,* rather than *blessing,* but for me the symbol of blessing is deeper and richer.

Alter says that he feels that the King James translation of Hebrew Scripture is truer to the intent of the original than any other. Other translations, in trying to avoid the frequent repetitions of the Hebrew, for instance, miss the point that these repetitions are a conscious artistic device, building in power. I read from many different translations, but I return again and again to the King James.

And I like it that Jacob is at last willing to give Esau a blessing.

Jacob and Esau were not either/or people. They had the full complexity of the both/and human being. Open at one moment, closed at another. Brave, cowardly. Loving, lying. Jacob never hesitated to cheat, and yet God called him Israel. How are we to understand?

We are at a demanding threshold of understanding right now, as we move from deterministic, forensic thinking, to more indeterministic, vulnerable thinking. We are unique, incomparable creatures, but was creating us God's chief achievement or ultimate aim? We can no longer separate ourselves from the rest of creation, nor think of ourselves as more important in

God's eyes than stars or butterflies or baboons. We are part of a whole which is so intricately balanced that the smallest action (watch that butterfly) can have cosmic consequences.

We need to step out of the limelight as being the pinnacle of God's work. I suspect that those first human creatures who walked upright on their hind legs and so freed their hands to make and use tools, most likely thought of themselves as the pinnacle of creation. Look at us! We are man who uses tools! God has done it at last!

Perhaps we have just as far to go in the long journey toward being truly human.

It is not easy to accept the both/and-ness of the people we love. Or ourselves. I am highly intelligent; I am also frequently extremely stupid. When somebody I love and admire does something which seems to me to be totally unworthy I am devastated, and it takes a while before I find balance and allow that person to be as both/and—or even more so—than I am. Sometimes it seems that the greater the human being, the deeper the potential for stupidity or sin.

I was brooding about this when a young friend of mine came to tell me that ultimately the computer will no longer be binary, but trinary. (A trinary [trinitarian] computer would not have "thought" I was leaving from Portland, Oregon.) Right now the computer works on the binary system: one/zero. Either/or. Yes/no. Lewis Carroll could have been forecasting our present computers when he had the Red Queen ask Alice, "What's one and one and one and one . . ."

When Alice says she doesn't have the faintest idea, the Red Queen says scornfully, "She can't do sums at all."

One and one and one and one . . . that's the way the computer counts, incredibly swiftly. But ultimately, even this is not going to be adequate. We are going to have to move to a computer which is trinary.

In technical language, my friend told me, the trinary computer will have positive polarity, negative polarity, and neutral polarity. Or: yes/no/*mu*. *Mu* means that neither yes nor no is a workable answer.

He illustrated this by a Zen koan. The Zen master asked his student to go to the nearby mountain and bring him the top mile. The student went to the master's study and brought him his pipe.

"What," my friend asked me, "is a *mu* answer to, 'Are you still beating your wife?'"

"I'm cooking chicken for dinner," I said.

And I thought that there are times in any marriage when, if one partner asks the other, "Do you love me?" neither yes nor no is a true reply. There are times when I don't love my husband. On the other hand, I don't *not* love him.

And there are times when that question should not be asked!

Jesus gave *mu* answers. When he was asked whether or not it was proper to pay tribute to Caesar, he said, "Bring me a coin."

A scribe said to Jesus, "Master, I will follow you wherever you go." A binary answer would have been, "Come with me," or "Go home." Jesus' trinary answer was, "The foxes have holes and the birds of the air have nests, but the son of man has no place to lay his head."

Occasionally other people responded to Jesus with trinary answers. He was brought a child who was possessed of an unclean spirit, and when the father begged for help, Jesus said, "If you can believe, all things are possible if you believe." And the child's father answered, "Lord, I believe. Help thou my unbelief."

When the disciples quarrelled over who was greatest among them, Jesus reached out and pulled a small child onto his lap.

When Nicodemus asked him, "Who is my neighbour?" Jesus told the story of the man set upon by thieves.

A man said to Jesus, "Master, speak to my brother and make

him divide our inheritance with me." And Jesus said, "Man, who made me a judge or divider over you?"

When the scribes and elders asked Jesus by whose authority he was preaching, he answered with another question, "The baptism of John, was it from heaven, or of men?"

(Oriental or occidental?)

Mu responses.

Often he replied with a story, and a story is usually *mu*. This is not an either/or, a yes/no. It is both/and/maybe.

Surely when Jacob fled from Esau's anger, and was given a vision of angels, that was not the yes or no that we human beings tend to expect. Angels, too, are *mu*.

A *mu* answer is redemptive, never destructive. It opens our eyes and ears. It helps us to be willing to move out of our comfortable rut, and to go out into the wilderness of questions which have no easy answers. How we long for easy answers and blanket statements. If we can label all problems, premarital sex, divorce, abortion, then we can safely refrain from thinking about the people who are suffering from these problems. Jesus made no blanket statements about social or political issues. Each person he met was given his focussed attention—the *person,* rather than the problem.

If you can label things, make blanket statements to cover all contingencies, you don't need symbols. Story is an alternative to labelling. Story is symbol.

Perhaps we human beings with our desire to label are very strange particles indeed. We live in a new world of radical change which is, nevertheless, as primitive in its own way as the world where Jacob poured oil on the stone he had used for a pillow, and proclaimed it to be the house of God.

Sometimes a new awareness of symbols is given along with small, unspectacular events. I spent a day with a group of men and women who had been through seminary and were ready to be ordained. One man, in his thirties, had read the *Time*

Trilogy the week before, and wanted to know why I had used so many occult references.

Occult references? I was baffled and a little shocked. I asked him to explain.

He mentioned the three Mrs W, Mrs Whatsit, Mrs Who, and Mrs Which. Especially Mrs Which. But—I thought the text made it quite clear that she (like the other two) is a guardian angel, and the name is a pun on which and witch, a play on words, and a deeper understanding of the godly possibility of the word. It has nothing to do with black magic or witchcraft. As Mrs Which herself remarks, when things are desperate we need to keep a sense of humour.

The young man thought the way I described Progo, the cherubim, as quirky and sometimes irritable might disturb people. But Progo is a very scriptural cherubim as I describe him, and it wouldn't surprise me a bit if those cherubim guarding the gates of Eden didn't get irritable on occasion. Was this young man thinking of renaissance cherubs, little baby heads with small, ineffectual wings? Hadn't he read (for instance) Ezekiel lately?

Then he asked me why I had used the dog, Ananda, as a familiar. Again, I was shocked. A familiar is an animal companion to a witch or warlock, frequently a black cat which talks, and gives the owner Satanic information. Ananda a familiar? Horrors! Ananda, who is joy, God's joy, could never be a familiar in the sense that the young man was using the word. That it was even possible for him to so misinterpret the story that he could think of a Satanic familiar in connection with this loving dog was appalling to me.

We do have a loving, kything relation with dogs; Ananda is not unlike one of our family dogs, Tyrrell, half Golden Retriever, half Shepherd, who had an unerring understanding of people. She was gentle, loving, affectionate. Like most Golden Retrievers she had a dolphin's smile. But she could smell wrongness. One time in the Cathedral Library I was introduced to a personable young man who was going to be working in the mail room. As he approached me, Tyrrell's hair bristled, and I heard a low, warning growl. Within the week the young man had stolen all the Cathedral keys and a large sum of money. I said, "Whenever Tyrrell is suspicious of someone, take the dog seriously." Tyrrell was a dog, a friend of human beings, guarding her people as best she could. She was not a "familiar."

Doc, my present Golden Retriever companion, has Tyrrell's nose for the psychotic. A Cathedral attracts people with problems and if Doc does not want someone to come into the library, and stays pressed close against me, I know that whoever it is has problems beyond my competence to handle. Often a listening ear is enough. Doc lets me know when more professional help is needed. Doc is a hurtling, golden rocket of love. She is not a "familiar."

Within the past year I have seen several articles on the need for many people to have pets, and that when someone with high blood pressure strokes a dog or a cat, the blood pressure is lowered. When the young man saw occult meanings in the *Time Trilogy*, what was he looking for?

Someone else in the group remarked that "occult" is not necessarily a bad word. It simply means "hidden."

It would certainly be possible to call the *Revelation* of Saint John the Divine "occult," for there is much in that extraordinary last book of the Bible that is hidden, and we show no evidence that we have come near to plumbing its depths.

I said that perhaps what I was inadvertently doing was hoping to redeem the symbols. The powers of darkness have no need to come where evil already is, but try to pervert the good. So I pray that my symbols were referring to the original good.

That is what we need to look for, the good in what God has created.

There is much that is hidden, and much of it is good and lovely and true. There is much in the life of Jesus that is hidden. We know almost nothing about him from the time when he spoke with the elders in the temple at the age of twelve, to the time when he began his adult ministry. There is much in our own selves, our own spirits, which is hidden, which only God knows. And there is much that we can understand only symbolically.

The new symbols created by the new physics are helpful to me in keeping my doors open. The butterfly effect; strange particles; or even particles that have a tendency to life (how alive are we?) and that are called virtual particles. And I do not want to forget the particles with the unusually long life-span of one millionth of a second.

The new symbols do not replace the old, but give them renewed vitality, so that they continue to inform my faith. Christ, small as a child, sitting on King David's lap. The small cross of the African bushman. The cup of salvation. Once again *chronos* and *kairos* intersect in the cross.

And yet, what about the cross? More and more crosses are being found today in churches where they would not have been tolerated a few decades ago. At the same time, the symbol has been weakened. The sign of the cross used to make the Devil take flight. A church was a sacred place of sanctuary. A thief who would rob a great house without compunction would not go into a church and touch the sacred vessels. Not so any more. At "my" Cathedral in New York, all the valuable crosses and candle sticks have had to be replaced with wood or ceramic ones, to prevent continuing theft. Great tapestries have been ripped from the high walls. Stones have been thrown through windows.

How do we reawaken a sense of the sacred?

First of all, we must look for it. Jacob fled Esau, and was given a vision of God. He was realistic about people, including himself, but he did not look for evil. So he was given the greatest good.

What are we looking for? For God and love and hope? Or for wrongness and evil and sin?

If the totally interdependent, interconnected world of physics is true, then this oneness affects the way we look at everything—books, people, symbols. It radically affects the way we look at the cross. Jesus on the cross was at-one with God, and with the infinite mind, in which Creation is held. The anguish on the cross has to do with this at-one-ment in a way which a forensic definition of atonement cannot even begin to comprehend.

For Jesus, at-one-ment was not being at-one only with the glory of the stars, or the first daffodil in the spring, or a baby's laugh. He was also at-one with all the pain and suffering that ever was, is, or will be. On the cross Jesus was at-one with the young boy with cancer, the young mother hemorrhaging, the raped girl. And perhaps the most terrible anguish came from being at-one with the people of Sodom and Gomorrah, the death chambers at Belsen, the horrors of radiation in the destruction of Hiroshima and Nagasaki. It came from being at-one with the megalomania of the terrorist, the coldness of heart of "good" people, or even the callous arrogance of the two men in criminal court.

We can withdraw, even in our prayers, from the intensity of suffering. Jesus, on the cross, experienced it all. When I touch the small cross I wear, that, then, is the meaning of the symbol.

May the Holy Spirit come and help all our symbols to be redeemed.

Echthroi
and
Angels
12

ON THE CROSS JESUS WAS AT ONE WITH GOD and the holy angels and rainbows and butterflies. And he was also, to his anguish, at one with Satan and all the fallen angels, with those who would viciously destroy what God has made with love and joy, with those whose pride is even greater than that of the terrorist. Because Jesus took into himself on the cross every evil and every sin and every brokenness to come upon this planet, there is the fragile but living hope that one day even Satan may once again join the sons of God when they gather round their Maker, and that he will beg to be allowed once again to carry the light. For, as Saint Paul wrote to the people of Philippi, "Every knee shall bow in heaven and on earth and under the earth, and every tongue confess that Jesus Christ is Lord, to the glory of the Father."

We know that the redemption of the cosmos is no easy matter. The actions of the dark angels are visible throughout Scripture, and even the protagonists of the stories bear the taint.

211

They lied; they cheated. They made great, inordinate demands of God, and in turn accepted the great and inordinate demands God threw at them. They looked at the stars and were given great promises, and their response may have been incredulity, but never indifference or smugness. They did wonderful things, and they did terrible things.

One of the stories related to that of Jacob which we seldom hear is the story of his daughter, Dinah. It is not a pleasant story, and we would rather forget it. But there it is.

Dinah, the daughter of Leah, the tender-eyed, "went out to meet the daughters of the land ... in Shalem, a city of Shechem, which is in the land of Canaan ... where Jacob, her father, had pitched his tent."

According to some translations, she was raped by Shechem, the son of Hamor the Hivite, prince of the country. However, the King James translation says that when Shechem saw her, "he took her, and lay with her, and defiled her. And his soul clave unto Dinah, the daughter of Jacob, and he loved the damsel."

That does not sound like rape. Shechem wanted to marry Dinah, because he loved her so much, and it would appear that Dinah wanted to marry him. However, no matter how it happened, he had defiled Dinah by lying with her before they were married, and her brothers were angry.

But Shechem told his father, the prince of the country, that he loved Dinah, and wanted her for his wife, and Hamor went to the sons of Jacob, saying, "The soul of my son Shechem longs for your daughter. I pray you, give her to him as wife, and all of you make marriages with us, and give your daughters to us, and take our daughters for yourselves. And you shall dwell with us, and our land shall be yours."

And Shechem said to Dinah's father, Jacob, and to her brothers, "Ask me for anything you want, and I will give you whatever it is you ask, only give me Dinah for my wife."

The sons of Jacob were still outraged because Shechem had defiled their sister, and they answered him deceitfully, telling him that they would give Dinah to him only if the Hivites would become as the Hebrews, and would circumcise every one of the males of their tribe.

The Jerusalem Bible says that Shechem "was the most important person in his father's household," and that he agreed to the circumcision. The King James translation reads, "And the young man deferred not to do this thing, because he had delight in Jacob's daughter, and he was more honourable than all the house of his father." I like to think that Shechem, despite his rash act, was a man of honour.

At any rate, all the male Hivites were circumcised, and on the third day, when they were still sore and in pain, Simeon and Levi, two of Leah's sons (and therefore Dinah's full brothers) took their swords and slew all the male Hivites. They killed Hamor and Shechem, and took Dinah out of Shechem's house. Then all the sons of Jacob pillaged the town and took everything—flocks, cattle, donkeys, children, wives (in that order).

Jacob was very upset by all of this, not so much the massacre, as the effect it would have on his reputation. He said to Simeon and Levi,

> You have done me harm, making me stink among the people of this land. There are many of them, and I have few in number, and they will gather themselves together against me, and slay me, and I shall be destroyed, I and my house.
>
> And Dinah's brothers said, "Should he deal with our sister as with a harlot?"
>
> And God said to Jacob, "Get up. Go to Beth-el [where Jacob had seen the ladder of angels uniting heaven and earth] and dwell there, and make there an altar [another altar!] unto God, who appeared to you when you were fleeing from your brother, Esau."

And Jacob told his household, "Get rid of all the strange gods you have with you, and wash, and change your clothes, and we will go to Beth-el."

And they gave Jacob all their strange gods. And all their ear rings.

It would still be a long time before El Shaddai would truly be understood as the God Who is One, the God Who is All.

It will still be a long time before we who call ourselves Christians will understand that God is One, that God is All, because we still worship many strange gods. When we set ourselves up as being the only people in Creation who have the truth and who will inherit the kingdom, we are worshipping the little god of our own pride.

When we greedily and proudly count the money we have taken in on a Sunday at church, or pride ourselves on the funds that we have sent into the mission field, we are in danger of worshipping the little gods of money and our own superiority.

When we divide ourselves into *us* and *them,* we court disaster.

I may be horrified and outraged when an assassination is committed in the name of religion, and when I discover a way of looking at God which is not mine, but I still may not separate myself from this horror with any sense of my own virtue. The butterfly's wings quiver with pain, and distant galaxies are shaken.

Is the killing of Gandhi, Martin Luther King, John or Robert Kennedy so different in essence from the killing of Hamor or Shechem?

There it is, the story of Dinah and her brothers, those brothers who would head the tribes of Israel. I don't know what to make of it, but I have to accept that it is part of the story—and that there is much to be learned from it.

This is all we know about Dinah. We are given no hint as to how *she* felt. Was she in love with Shechem? Between the lines, I sense that she was. But she, along with Shechem, had broken the taboo, and retribution followed.

Later on in history, when Moses the lawgiver came into the story, a woman who had committed adultery was to be stoned—stoned to death. The fault, according to the law, seemed to lie more with the woman than with the man. At least Dinah was spared stoning.

When Joseph first learned that Mary was pregnant, he should have given her over to be stoned to death, according to the law. What an extraordinary man he was! He was willing to by-pass the law by putting Mary away quietly. And then, even more remarkable, he was able to accept the words of the angel, that the child—the holy seed—in Mary's womb had been sown there by the Holy Spirit.

What was Joseph looking for? Not anger, not retribution, not even justice, but love.

"What are you looking for?" Jesus asked the people.

There are, praise the Lord, only a few Christians who are hoping to find those who are less Christian than they are, in order to feel superior by contrast. There are only a few people who are reading books looking for pornography, or counting the number of dirty words rather than reading the story. There are far many more people who are truly looking for God, however and wherever the Creator may choose to reveal the divine nature. There are many more people who are looking for the revelation of infinite compassion in Christ.

We do find what we look for. Or do we? In a way, yes. But it's not quite that easy. Pilgrim struggled a long way from the wicket gate to the Celestial City. If we are looking for love, that is what we will find. But love never promised there would be no suffering. Love never promised to stop all the attacks of the echthroi. Love led Jesus to the cross, rather than sparing him.

Echthroi is a word which I first used in the *Time Trilogy*. It is a Greek word, meaning *the enemy.* It is an enemy-sounding word. *Echthroi* is the plural noun; *echthros* is the singular. The echthroi are those who would separate us from the stars and each other, un-Name, annihilate. The fallen angels are echthroi, and so are disease and famine and hate and vanity and a host of other little nasty things. The echthroi would teach us despair, indifference, would have us believe that unmerited suffering is deliberately inflicted on the creature by an angry Creator. The echthroi are forensic. They are powerful. But love is greater.

I spent nearly a week at Holy Cross monastery, to teach a writers' workshop, followed by a weekend retreat. At the end of a hard day's work, my old bones need to soak in a hot tub. Because the only room in the monastery with a tub, not a shower, is in the monastic enclosure, I was allowed to sleep there. Was I the first female to sleep in this all male bastion? The cell I was in has been slept in by bishops, missionaries, preachers, from all over the world. It is likely that many spiritual battles have been fought within its white walls.

I was struggling with something minor, a nasty cold which had been hanging on for weeks, giving me a bronchial cough and fever, and I was finally on antibiotics to help me through the workshop and the retreat. Kind people gave me cough drops and vitamin C, and one of the monks loaned me a heavy cape in which to wrap myself, and another gave me his bottle of cough medicine.

The third night I was there I had a dream in the early hours of the morning. It was very cold, and the cold had wakened me, and I lay there, trying to warm up and go back to sleep, saying the Jesus Prayer: "Lord Jesus Christ, have mercy on me." Then there was a sense of pressure by me, of someone, some-*thing* on the bed, and then there was a feeling of terrible evils battling, and I clung frantically to the Jesus Prayer, calling it out, over and over: "Lord Jesus Christ, have mercy on me." Then it seemed to me that although I was caught in the great winds of horrible evil, I was not the target, I was simply in the path of the storm, and I kept calling out the prayer, until the storm was over. In my dream a monk came in, which seemed quite natural, and pointed out the evidence of the storm. The wallpaper had been stripped from the far wall, and the plaster beneath was violently pockmarked.

What I told the monk was that this horrible episode proved to me that my faith in Jesus Christ was really real, and that had I not been holding on to the name of Jesus, the storm of evil would have killed me, and Christ truly was, is, salvation.

This was Epiphany Eve—when Christians celebrate God's revelation of love to all humankind. What a marvellous showing forth!

The transition from sleeplessness to the dream was seamless, and so was the transition from the dream to being awake, alone in an untouched room. So real had it been that it took a while for me to realize that it had been a dream. I looked at the far wall, and there was no wall paper, only smooth, unpocked plaster.

The amazing thing is that as I looked back at the dream it was not a "bad" dream, or a nightmare; it was a glorious affirmation of the power of Christ. The storm of evil had not only not put out the light, it was proof that the light was there and the light could not be extinguished.

The echthroi, quite logically, attack the Good. Saint Anthony in the desert (the same desert on which Jacob pitched his tent) was attacked by all kinds of venomous demons. In the past year or so the attacks seem to have become more frequent and more vicious all over the world. Drawing back in fear is more dangerous than staying in the vanguard, but that does not make the echthroid attacks any less terrible.

In the past few months I have had more calls than I want to count asking for prayers—prayers for good people who have been stricken with cancer, multiple sclerosis, terrible accidents. Why?

Why, if we find what we look for, why do terrible things

happen to people who are looking for good, and who serve the good?

That question has never been answered. It is asked, one way or another, all through the Old Testament. The entire book of Job grapples with it, but gives no definitive answer. Yet, underlying the lack of an answer is an unspoken affirmation that ultimately all shall be well.

God is still the author of the story, and even if the echthroi tear and crumple the pages, or smudge the ink, it is still God's story, and the Author will correct, revise, retype, redeem, as necessary. Meanwhile, we are part of the story, and we may not know what the lines we are given mean, why we suffer, bleed, die. Perhaps what we see as death is really necessary for rebirth.

Recently I was negotiating a contract for a movie of one of my books, *The Arm of the Starfish*. The problem with the standard Hollywood contract is that it has a clause giving the producer freedom to change character and theme. Not only can I not sign that clause, the contract must reverse it. I became aware of the absurdity of the Hollywood legal mind when, in the contract for *A Wrinkle in Time* (where that nasty clause had been reversed), I was to grant rights to the work in perpetuity throughout the universe! I took a red pen, made a °, and wrote, "with the exception of Sagittarius and the Andromeda galaxy." They actually accepted it. And I was told later that there was considerable discussion about this. Could I possibly know something about Sagittarius and the Andromeda galaxy that they didn't know?

Will *Wrinkle* be made into a movie? Supposedly. But there are times when I think it is more likely to happen on Andromeda galaxy than here. We'll see.

Meanwhile, in discussions with the potential producers of *Starfish*, we had to make clear what I would and what I would not allow to be changed. We all agreed that it needs updating.

The world of the eighties is very different from the world of the sixties, when the book was written.

It was suggested that Adam, the young protagonist, would not be apt to carry secret papers; it would more likely be some kind of microchip. All right.

"What about Adam and Kali?" I was asked. "Wouldn't their relationship go a little further?"

I had to agree that now, twenty years later, it probably would. The word *relationship* wasn't even in our vocabulary twenty years ago. We used to have friendship, and love.

"Does Joshua have to die?" I was then asked.

"Yes."

"Why?"

"Because that's what happened," I said firmly.

"But Joshua was *good.*"

"Yes," I agreed.

"But doesn't *good* imply *protection?*"

"No," I said. No. And then it came to me that the only one who has ever offered protection is Satan. That was one of the temptations given to Jesus on the mountain after his baptism. Worship me, Satan urged him, and you can have it all free, no being deserted by the disciples you had counted on to stay with you, no cross, no pain, no suffering. I will protect you.

But does the God of love not offer that kind of protection?

Again I am caught in paradox and contradiction.

I have on occasion been blessed by extraordinary miracles of healing. At other times, not. Why does God miraculously cure one person, and allow another to die in agony? Why does one child appear to be under the protection, while another is struck by a drunken driver?

Why? There are no easy answers. The easy answers, such as a predetermined universe, do not seem compatible with a God of love.

And yet—

I have been offered prayers of protection, and I believe in them. But they are not magic. Magic is manipulation. Prayers for protection are not.

It helps a little if I think of myself as a human parent. My deepest desire is to protect my children. My lioness instinct toward my cubs is great. But I cannot offer my children complete protection. We may want to make everything all right for our children, but we cannot. All we can do is love them, and help them grow up. We have to let the baby struggle to its feet and fall, and stand again, and fall again, as it learns to walk. All during our children's lives we have to let them learn to walk alone, to let go the hand. The over-protected child becomes incapable of growing into a mature human being. We must allow our children to be themselves, not manipulated appendages of their parents. We can try to give them standards, to teach by example, and we hope they will use the standards in resisting the many temptations they will be offered, but we can't resist the temptations for them; they have to resist for themselves. God did not resist the temptations for Jesus; Jesus had to confront Satan alone.

Satan, Lord of the echthroi. The enemy of Christ. The enemy of each one of us. Of the cosmos.

But Satan did not come from outside the cosmos. He was one of the sons who met with God at the beginning of the book of Job. He was the beautiful angel Lucifer—the light bearer—who thought he could do it all better than God. Just look at life here on this planet; what a mess it is! Christians killing in the name of Christ, hardness of heart, famine, drought, greed, filth, inequity, imbalance. Don't we all think we could have done a better job of it? Satan certainly thought he could. And he is tempting us, assuring us, "You are better than the others, better than *them*," and we fall for it all too often.

"It must have been so hard on Michael," my friend Sister

Mary Michael said, "when he had to fight Lucifer, because they were best friends."

Is it possible for them to be best friends again, at the end of time, when Satan no longer wants to do it all himself, and is willing to return to the joy of interdependence? That is what I hope for and desire. I equally hope for reconciliation for many estranged friends, parents and children, brothers and sisters, for churches split apart by discord over trivialities, for races isolated from each other because of a sense of superiority. And there *is* hope. Listen to St. Paul again, in Colossians 1:

> For in Christ all the fullness of God was pleased to dwell, and through him to reconcile to himself all things, whether on earth, or in heaven, making peace by the blood of his cross. And you, who once were estranged and hostile in mind, doing evil deeds, he has now reconciled in his body of flesh by his death . . .

Sometimes when I am working my way through a Bach fugue I hear strange dissonances before ultimately the theme emerges, triumphant. The dissonances, rather than spoiling the fugue, make the working out of the theme more beautiful. Bach was criticized for some of the strange discordancies in his music, but the ending always resolved all discord into harmony.

If it is difficult to understand that sin and evil come from within Creation, rather than from without, a look at our own bodies, our own inner selves, can be helpful. Few of us have bodies of flawless perfection, yet we would not throw away the body because of nearsighted eyes, weak ankles. When I have a fever or hurt myself, I pray for my body's healing. Our thoughts are not always pure and loving, but when I feel resentful or self-pitying, these unhappy qualities come from within me, not without me. And I pray that my ill-feelings will be turned to healthy, loving ones. At the Second Coming, when all things are redeemed, then we, like all of creation, will know wholeness and holiness through Christ, "who will change our lowly body to be like his glorious body, in the power which enables him even to subject all things to himself"—Paul's radical affirmation.

Meanwhile we pray that we will be given our own parts to play in healing the fragments which separate us dis-astrously. In anguish we pray for the healing of the universe, for as long as any part of Creation is in rebellion, all of it cries in pain. "If one member suffers, all suffer together; if one member is hon-ored, all rejoice together." And then Paul moves into "a still more excellent way," the way of Love in his first letter to the people of Corinth. It is not easy to understand that love is the most powerful of all weapons, love in its very weakness.

How do we bless the echthroi? When they attack (and surely they have been attacking) I call on the angels.

When Jacob wrestled with the angel he understood that the angel was not only a messenger of God, but an aspect of God. When I call on the angels, I feel that I am calling on Christ, in whose service the angels perform their works.

Jesus taught us that God is love; so what am I calling the angels to do when the enemy attacks, leaving pain and grief and bitter tears?

I have had to move from thinking that the echthroi have to be killed by God's avenging angels, to wondering whether they, like the rest of creation, may be redeemed and blessed. Turned from despair to hope. Changed even more radically than Paul was changed, so that they may no longer be destroying angels, but angels of light. The symbol of the avenging angel itself has to be transformed. The two-edged sword is no longer a weapon of death, but of healing.

Big words. Yes. And I mean these big words. But how? It would be obscene to get sentimental about the "poor" echthroi, poor though they may be.

It is not difficult for me to want those two defendants, whom

I observed while I was on jury duty, to be healed and redeemed from their own evil. After all, they didn't hurt me. This hope for a blessing might not even be too difficult for the feisty old woman they'd attacked; after all, they had succeeded only in nicking her with their knives.

But what about the parents whose only daughter has been raped and then stabbed to death? Granted, the "Christian duty" is for them to pray for the murderer's redemption. But this kind of holiness doesn't come without terrible anger to be gone through, without terrible pain. "Though we went through fire and water," the psalmist sings to the Lord, "we have not forgotten you." Was such anger and pain the fire and water to which the psalmist referred?

Esau has something to teach us here. "Bless me, too, oh, my father, bless me, too." And he walked through fire and water and forgave Jacob.

What greater grief could any woman have than Eve? Her younger son, Abel, was dead. Her elder son, Cain, had killed him. With all the empathy of which I am capable, I cannot imagine the intensity of such anguish.

And yet God came into this world as one of us, not to destroy, but to heal. To redeem. To bless.

A friend of mine in the Midwest showed me an article on a possible new and very different way of treating cancer. Instead of trying to kill the cancer cells, the new hope of cure is to turn the malignant cells back into normal, benign cells, to change them from being destroyers into cells which once again play their own essential interdependent part in the functioning of the body. If Paul Brand is right in saying that cancer cells are the only cells in the body which insist on being autonomous, with no concern for the other cells they destroy, then our hope is that it will ultimately be possible for them to be transformed, and returned to the creative interdependence of normal cells.

So we must seek to change the echthroi from being destroyers, as cancer cells are destroyers; we must hope to see them changed into holy angels once again, each with a unique but interdependent role in the working out of the fulfillment of the cosmos.

How do we very human creatures help change the fallen angels into the radiance of love again? Of course, it is nothing we can do of ourselves at all, but the more we open ourselves to the holy angels, the less room there is for the fallen ones.

If I remain stuck in a groove of self-pity, if I insist on vindication, I am opening myself to the echthroi. We all want justice, but if we demand it at the price of love it will be dark justice indeed. I pray, fumblingly, for those who have hurt me, for those I have hurt, for those who have been attacked by the echthroi. Not a demanding prayer, just an offering of a timid hope of love. Neither coercion nor manipulation are effective in turning anyone toward Christ. Coercion and manipulation only *add* to the pain of the cross. My prayer is simply a holding out of whoever it is, friend or foe, to the love of God. That implies that I am willing, reluctantly or no, to accept some of the cross. If I hold out in prayer a teen-age boy dying of leukemia, I cannot do it without accepting some of the anguish of the parents, the confusion of the siblings, the thrust toward life and then the letting go of the boy himself.

If I try to hold up in prayer the friend whose life is radically changed because of a love shattered and killed, I cannot do it without being part of the wounds and the anger. To hold someone lovingly in my hands, my hands held out to God, is to share, even in an infinitesimally tiny way, some of the agony of the cross. Blessing is not easy, and it cannot be reversed.

The promise is that not only can we bear the dark night, but that dawn will come.

For, as Paul said to the people of Rome, ". . . the creation itself will be set free from its bondage to decay and obtain the glorious liberty of the children of God . . . We know that the whole creation has been groaning in travail together until now; and not only the creation, but we ourselves . . . But if we hope for what we do not see, we wait for it with patience."

And then it is time to move from those close to me, or known to me personally, to the powers of darkness themselves.

Bless the bastard.

Bless the echthroi . . .

How? By holding them out to the love of God.

Make no mistake. This is no permissive, wishy-washy, cozy love. The best of us will be burned by it. Malachi warned that this love "is like a refiner's fire, and like fullers' soap; and . . . shall . . . purge them as gold and silver, that they may offer unto the Lord an offering in righteousness." It may take eons before self-will is diminished enough so that we want this terrible purging. And for the echthroi, the fallen angels, it will be terrible indeed.

But that is God's part in it. What is ours?

Simply to bless, no matter how ungraciously. To begin with blessing the easily identified echthroi: disease, terrorists, rapists, powermongers. Then keep coming in closer. Hold out to the love of God those who have hurt us. Those who have let us down. Who, for one reason or another, slap out at us, put us down, reject us. Those whose forgiveness we must accept when we have done any of these things ourselves.

Those we encounter in our daily lives, family, friends, people we pass on the street. And I had to think about those two defendants on the jury duty case whose clever lawyers managed to dance legalistic circles around the more straightforward assistant district attorney. Those two men were guilty, but they were charged with more injury than they actually inflicted. The intent to injure or kill was there but the result was not. Therefore, according to the law, and according to the charge, the assistant district attorney did not prove them guilty beyond a reasonable doubt.

We jurors spent at least an hour during our deliberation trying to find a loophole in the defending lawyers' cleverness, to find a way where we could legitimately avoid saying Not Guilty but, according to the law, we could not. The judge had told us that in England a jury can bring in a verdict of "Not proven guilty," and that is what we would like to have done. But we had to say "Not Guilty," because this is the American way, and we felt heavy about it, but not nearly as heavy as we would have felt in a judicial system where guilt is assumed, rather than having to be proved.

Bless the brutes. With the blessing, help them to see that their brutality hurts them as much as the old woman they attacked. Bless them so that they may turn from the echthroi, turn their anger and violence and resentment to the light of love for healing.

"God bless you, sir," Jerome Hines said to Khrushchev.

Oh, God will indeed bless, but we must play our own part in the blessing.

Pope John Paul II played his part when he was willing to talk, lovingly, with his would-be assassin.

St. Stephen played his part when he asked that his murderers' action not be held against them.

Mozart, composing the grief-filled and yet joyous Requiem Mass, was playing his part.

* * *

Then it's time to move in even closer. To call on God to bless and transform the enemy within ourselves. (Remembering that a blessing once given can never be retracted.)

Only if I am able to bless the parts of myself which are furthest from God's image, are these objectionable parts redeemable. How do I go about this blessing? It is not easy, I am often too hurt or too angry to have the least desire to bless. Yet, ultimately, I know that the blessing must be given in a context of love, not my own love, but that of other people, my husband, my family, my friends, who allow me to be complex and contradictory. Who thereby bless me. I cannot do it myself! I can only pray that it will be done.

* ✳ *

Are there people who have been so damaged by lack of having been given love, or having been so manipulated or corrupted by the self-serving sham that masquerades as love, that they are beyond the possibility of blessing, or knowing themselves blessed?

I'm not sure. At least, there are those who, in this life, are wounded spiritually beyond relief. But God will not give up. Nor need we, though we must bless with a full awareness that we may not succeed. In the view of the world, Jesus did not succeed. But the world, and often the church, puts expectations of success on us which are such burdens that they can become a form of cursing. It should be only the echthroi who tempt us by making us believe that our love, in human terms, ought not to fail. But it does—often it does. Yet that need not stop love from growing.

Those echthroi within us: can I always tell what they are? Sometimes it's easy. Self-pity, jealousy, resentment, are echthroid. But often it is not possible to tell whether something is good or bad, virtue or vice. We cannot take a pad and draw a line down the middle, and then list our good qualities on one side, our bad on the other. What is good in one situation may not be good at all in another. And vice versa. I am very stubborn, nay, pigheaded, which can be very hard on those I love. On the other hand, during those long years of rejection slips for writing that I believed in, it was that very pigheadedness which kept me going. It has helped me "hang in there" in other times of crisis, too. So the very flaw of stubbornness can be a blessing. And ultimately, all shall be blessed, all the wounds and cracks in the universe.

There is an enormous difference between wallowing in our own brokenness and sense of sin, and in accepting it, and then turning to the Lamb for a transfusion. There is an enormous difference between seeing ourselves as virtuous and morally correct, so that therefore anything we do is permissible and innocent, and recognizing ourselves as God's children, loved simply because we *are*.

I suspect that those who would look for Satan-worshippers instead of fellow companions journeying to Christ, that the terrorists with their holy fanaticism, that those who would curse, wipe out, unName, do other than bless, are all caught in *chronos*, bound by time. When Lucifer and the fallen angels refused to bear the light, they also refused God's time, *kairos*. The prince of this world and his cohorts reign in time, limited time. They are fearful, for the winds of the Holy Spirit are blowing, and so the attack is accelerating. As we look around our war-torn planet, our own disturbed and dissatisfied country, the echthroi appear to be making more progress than the angels.

But they are not. They are not.

They have been around the planet ever since the serpent offered Eve the apple. But their victories are hollow.

Terrible things happen, as in the story of Dinah and her brothers, in which the echthroi surely had their part, but God's blessing is more powerful than the echthroi's cursing.

This is something we cannot truly know until it has been tested.

Did I really mean it when I told the movie producer that being good implies no protection? Yes. Accepting Christ as Lord implies no protection, not in mortal terms. Nothing is guaranteed. No one is immune.

I was told a horrible story about a good Christian family.

One afternoon the mother is giving the baby a bath. The doorbell downstairs rings, shrilly, urgently. She rushes to answer it. Her older child follows her, trips, falls down the stairs and breaks his neck. She opens the door to be told that her husband has just been killed in an accident at work. Upstairs the baby drowns in the tub.

How can we react to such horrors except "curse God and die"?

Why don't we?

I have been praying during these past months for several people with multiple tragedies. Ma Katzenjammer in the old comics used to say, "Too much is enough." It seems not to be so.

In my own small way—and it is *very* small, merely inconvenient, not tragic—I am witness to the fact that we cannot say when enough becomes too much. 1984 was not a good year for my body. In January, I came down with shingles. One does not wish shingles on one's worst enemy. This was followed by a crashing fall on Broadway, when I tripped over a puppy who was terrified of city noises and ran between my legs. As my face hit the sidewalk, my dark glasses frame hit my cheekbone, and I had a haematoma which would make Lon Chaney in one of his worst roles look pretty. Hugh said, "If this was TV, they'd send you to makeup to take some off."

Then there was a weird virus which manifested itself with stabbing pains in the head, and finally, after giving me a couple of weeks of acute discomfort, faded away. Then there was the aeromonas with its painful cramping and bleeding. And then, when my body's resistance was low because I was just off steroids for the aeromonas, I came down with the current bronchial cold which continued all through December and into January. But it was *last* year's cold. I couldn't blame it on the new year, 1985, which I superstitiously counted on to do better by me.

On the second Sunday of January, I went for a walk in the woods around Crosswicks with three young friends. I knew that there was ice under the snow, so I wore my stoutest boots, took a stick, and my friends confirmed the fact that I was being very careful indeed. Careful or no, all of a sudden my feet went out from under me, and I crashed down on a rock.

One young friend said, later, "When you just lay there and didn't move, I knew something bad had happened."

It had. I'd broken my right shoulder. We were quite a distance from home, and I said, "Don't touch me, please. Don't touch my arm. Just let it hang." That, it happened, was the best thing I could have done, because the weight of the arm provided its own traction, and by the time it was x-rayed in the hospital, the bones were in place. It also happened that the orthopedist I wanted was on call that Sunday.

In the emergency room I said to him, "In just over a week I have to be in Chapel Hill, North Carolina." He looked at me and raised his eyebrows. Then he proceeded to truss me up in a shoulder-immobilizer.

Shoulder-immobilizers were designed by a man, for people with flat chests. If anybody wants to get rich and retire early, I suggest designing a female shoulder-immobilizer for people like me, who do *not* have flat chests.

I went home, helpless and hurting. And angry. I had not been careless. I had not caused myself to fall. I called my friend, Tallis, and told him that I had been pushed by an echthros, and no, I was not trying to be funny.

Nevertheless, is there anything to do except laugh? Such an accumulation inevitably becomes comic. I, however, did not find it humourous in the least. For the first few days the pain was excruciating (People who have had shingles get the idea when I tell them that it hurt worse than shingles).

I wept.

Who was I to think that a year of bodily vicissitudes was enough? Very clever, echthroi, tempting me into this kind of superstition. Very funny, tripping me up like that.

No, I don't think God willed my broken shoulder. God does not want pain for his creatures. But whatever happens, God will come into it and use it for good. I cried a lot the first couple of days. I hurt a lot. But it wasn't long before I began to see God's blessing in the midst of the pain of the shoulder and the discomfort of the masculine shoulder-immobilizer, which still makes me growl.

To keep myself sane, I struggled to type with my left hand. Holding a pen or pencil was impossible. But, even the day after the accident, I could sit at the typewriter for short periods of time, the electronic typewriter so sensitive to touch that it calls for almost no muscle expenditure. Of course I made all kinds of typographical errors with my clumsy left hand, but at least I could do a little work, and that was a needed affirmation. The echthroi hadn't completely conquered me; I was still human.

When I wasn't attempting to type with the left hand, I lay in bed, propped high on pillows, so that gravity could continue to provide traction for the broken humerus and shoulder. Usually I sleep flat, but I had to learn to sleep sitting up.

Now that we live in New York for much of the year, we can no longer take an active part in village life. I go to the church where once I directed the choir. But I am not there regularly enough even to sing in the choir. We left our tight-knit little community twenty-five years ago when we moved from the village back to New York.

But the day after I broke my shoulder I discovered that the old support system was still there, and still working. Somehow or other, as happens in a village, news of my fall got around. The phone rang. It was Eunice. "I'm sending dinner over tonight. Bernie will bring your dinner tomorrow." Martha, recovering from a serious operation, called to see how I was.

After twenty-five years!

And once again I was part of the church at work.

And the bride was beautiful.

After all, I did go to Chapel Hill, to Aqueduct Conference Center, started by the evangelist, Tommy Tyson, who quickly became a healing friend. Tommy has a strong healing ministry, and the first evening he anointed me with oil, put his hands on me, and prayed for healing. I think he was a little disappointed the next morning that there was no dramatic and visible result. But I told him, truthfully, that indeed I could feel healing.

And the truth of this was borne out six months later. I had been warned by my doctor that the break was so severe that I would not regain the full mobility and strength of the right arm. At the final visit he had me raising both arms, reaching behind my back, moving in every direction, and at last he said, "Which shoulder was it?" And then, "I wouldn't have believed it!"

Progress came in steps: the first joy was when I could hold a pen in my hand and write. The second was when I began to play the piano for therapy, at first miserably, but then with more and more freedom. And a great day came when I could fasten my bra in back again!

Granted, I worked very hard at rehabilitation, but I did it at home. I did not have physiotherapy, because the doctor said that I was doing the exercises myself. I met two women who had broken their shoulders and had not regained their mobility and were unable to carry anything heavy, and I was determined I was not going to have a crippled arm. But all the determination in the world cannot do everything. I had Tommy's prayers, and I had the prayers of other loving friends. And I am grateful. Thank you, Tommy. Thank you, Spirit of Love.

Hugh was free to go to North Carolina with me, otherwise I could not have made it. I was, indeed, physically helpless. I could talk, which was the main thing expected of me at Aqueduct, but that's about all. Believe me, a broken shoulder doesn't immobilize only the shoulder. It was painfully difficult for me to get on and particularly *off* the toilet, so the doctor suggested a toilet seat extender, a large plastic insert which raises the seat six or so inches, and which made an incredible amount of difference. I told Hugh, wistfully, that I would really need this plastic extender in North Carolina, so he went back to the store where he had bought it, and asked for a cardboard box. The only available box was marked in large black letters: ADULT INCONTINENT PADS. So off we went to the airport with a suitcase, and a large cardboard box packed with the toilet seat extender, books, and clothes.

Ever since Hugh retired from his TV show I had been trying unsuccessfully to get him to do readings with me. I think he realized that being nothing but a nursemaid at Aqueduct wouldn't be a good idea, so he agreed to do the readings, and we started each session with dramatic readings from one or another of my books, and he was a tremendous success. Everybody thought he was marvellous—as indeed he was.

We were together on our 39th anniversary on January 26th, 1985, only because he was with me at the conference. In the morning he was washing me, since I still couldn't do even that much for myself, and he remarked, "Who would have thought, thirty-nine years ago, that this is what we'd be doing today!"

One morning Carolyn, the hostess at the conference center, brought me in a cup of coffee. Hugh was sacrificing himself by eating in the dining hall with all the women, and Hugh is not chatty in the morning, and the acoustics emphasized his deafness. But he went, and he was gracious, and loved. And I said, "Carolyn, all kinds of blessings have come about because Hugh is at this conference with me, but did God need to break my shoulder to do this?"

Carolyn simply smiled and said, "Madeleine, God didn't break your shoulder. He's just using it."

Of course. But at that moment I needed blessed Carolyn to articulate it for me. God does not cause any of the bad things that happen, but God can take anything and redeem it. We still ask why terrible things happen to good people, why a loving God can allow war and illness and accident and death. We still grapple with the thorny problem of a loving God who has given his people the terrible gift of free will. Over and over again we abuse that gift, but God can come into whatever it is, and make it new.

God didn't cause me to fall and break my shoulder. I didn't cause it, either. It was an accident. It happened. And God came into it and used it for good.

Not long after the week in North Carolina, the United States Information Agency had made plans to send me, as a cultural representative, across Egypt and Austria. By then I was able to do a little bit more for myself, but not much, and I certainly couldn't have travelled alone, so Hugh went with me, and again, we did readings, to all kinds of groups, in Cairo and Heliopolis and Alexandria, in Vienna and Klagenfurt and Salzburg, a fascinating experience for both of us. What we were aiming for with our readings and our conversations was to make connections, to affirm that the things which unite human beings are more central than the things which separate us, and we did indeed make connections, and find at-one-ness, and we made friends—friends to be treasured all our lives. And we have continued to give readings together.

Someone said to me, "It was worth breaking your shoulder, wasn't it?"

And I replied, "Well, I can't quite go *that* far." But many blessings came out of the pain and the helplessness. And a new understanding of God's loving concern for us, the children.

This loving concern did not spare Jesus from the temptations. God did not stop the disciples from betraying him, or the Romans from crucifying him. But God offered Jesus, and offers us, the one protection that Satan does not give: *God is in it with us.* The God of love, unlike Satan, does not stand aside and look on suffering, unmoved. God is part of it, and because of that, we are given strength to bear things we did not think we could possibly bear. And because God is in it with us, our souls are helped to grow strong and to mature.

God does not want, or cause, the bad things to happen. But with God's patient and unfaltering love, they can be redeemed.

* ✳ *

So did I really mean it when I said in the discussion of a movie of *The Arm of the Starfish* that there is, in mortal terms, no protection?

Yes. Only Satan can give us mortal protection, but what kind of protection is that? Satan can offer great length of years, but only in these mortal bodies. He cannot offer us the real body, the pre-Fall body, the resurrection body. Satan can probably find us parking places, keep us from getting colds, even protect us from bullets, and bombs, and cancer. But the only protection worth having is something Satan cannot give: oneness with God.

Satan fractured the original oneness when he took himself and his fellow echthroi and rebelled against Love. Even when, on the surface, Satan protects, his chief mission is to continue to break, fragment, separate. Satan never offers himself, except as an object for abject worship.

If our worship of God means anything at all, it must be voluntary, not coerced. Satan will bargain with us. God (as Jacob discovered) will not. What God does offer is the Presence itself. Whatever it is, God is part of it, working to heal that which is broken, put together all the shards and fragments. God is with us in all our pain and grief and confusion, sharing, being, redeeming. This love does not stop with our deaths. That is the Christian affirmation. We do not ever stop being part of God's plan, part of the Unity, part of the work of the coming of the Kingdom, when all shall be made new.

I need to reiterate here what is a basic affirmation for me. When the world was created, as the story is told in the beginning of Genesis, God did not say, "It is finished." That did not come until the Cross. What God said after making the world was, "It is Good. It is very Good."

In March I saw my newborn grandson, a gorgeous, beautiful baby. Complete. Perfect. But finished? No! Anything but finished!

As this baby's parents are going to have the joy of watching him grow and develop and mature, so it is God's joy still to be part of Creation. And it is our calling to share in that loving creativity, to be willing to be open to change, to new revelation, new growth, as we are offered opportunities to go on with the work of that Creation which is called very good. I do not know why these opportunities are so often given us through the things which hurt us, or even kill us, but God knows, and that is all that is necessary.

When I receive Communion, when I am given the strengthening bread, the transfusion of the wine, this is the great symbol of God's oneness with Creation, the ultimate protection, God in us; we in God.

It is enough.

✳ ✳ ✳

Immediately after his sons' horrible slaughter of Shechem and the Hivites, Jacob left that place, and went to "Luz, which is in the land of Canaan, that is, Beth-el [where he had seen the glorious ladder], he and all the people that were with him. And he built there an altar, and called the place El-Beth-el; because there God appeared unto him."

Deborah, Rebekah's nurse, died (she must have been very

old), and was buried there under an oak tree.

And God appeared unto Jacob again, and blessed him. "And God said to him, your name is Jacob; you shall not be called Jacob any more, but Israel shall be your name."

So they moved from Beth-el toward Ephrath, and were nearly there, nearly to the place which would later be identified with Bethlehem, "and Rachel travailed, and she had hard labour." In giving birth to Benjamin, Rachel died, and was buried on the way to Ephrath, which is Bethlehem.

"And Jacob set a pillar upon her grave, and that is the pillar of Rachel's grave to this day."

Next we come to another difficult part of the story. Reuben, Jacob's eldest son, "went and lay with Bilhah, his father's concubine." Bilhah was one of the maids who had given sons to Jacob—Bilhah, Rachel's maid. Jacob heard what Reuben, his son, had done. It was the breaking of a taboo, and Reuben was to suffer for it. Yet it was Reuben who prevented the rest of the brothers from killing their braggart younger brother, Joseph. Reuben, like all scriptural heroes, was complex. But he had compassion, and for that I like him.

Jacob returned at last to Isaac, his father.

And chronology shudders.

When Jacob stole Esau's blessing from his father, the old man seemed to have been on his death bed, his eyesight gone with age, urging his son to come to him with a savoury stew to give him strength that he might give his blessing before he died. And here it was, more than twenty years later. Either the biblical narrator is playing very free and easy with chronology, or Isaac had the longest death-bed scene in history. But biblical time is not linear, like our chronology in the Western world. If King David could hold Christ on his lap (and of course he could) why shouldn't Isaac be alive when the narrator needs him?

"Isaac was one hundred and four score years, and he gave

up the ghost, and was gathered unto his people, being full of days, and his sons Esau and Jacob buried him."

And though Jacob and Esau were thoroughly reconciled, they had both acquired so many flocks and herds that the land could not support them both, so they parted their ways.

Jacob, through tears and laughter, had learned something of God's promise. He had demanded a blessing; he had demanded protection. And God had blessed him, but had not given him the protection Jacob had tried to bargain for. God blessed Jacob and made him vulnerable. His beloved Rachel died in childbirth. His elder son betrayed him with Rachel's maid, Bilhah, who had given him children. He was to think for many years that his favourite son, Joseph, was dead.

Still he loved God, although he never understood the nature of El Shaddai, but that didn't seem to matter very much.

He learned not only that God gives us the gift of vulnerability, but also the gift of pain, instead of the affliction of the absence of pain.

How do we tell the echthroi from the true angel (like the great one who wrestled with Jacob all night)? How do we join with God's holy angels in loving the fallen ones so that they may become light-bearers again? How do we continue the blessing of Jacob through our own lives?

Jesus came into the world to save sinners, to look for the lost sheep, to heal the blind, and deaf, and dumb, and leprous, and those possessed by demons, to give hope to the wounded and bleeding and broken. And Jesus came to fulfill the prophecy and go to the Cross and break the barriers of time and space in the mighty act of at-one-ment with all of Creation.

God does not promise us protection any more than he promised it to Jesus. Or Jacob. We are not given protection. We are given vulnerability.

We are promised not the absence of pain, but the blessed warning of pain.

238

We are promised not that we won't be wounded, that we won't bleed, but that we will be transfused.

We are promised not that we won't die, but that we shall live.

*   ✳   *

What must Jacob have felt, after Rachel's death, when he held baby Benjamin in his arms, the baby whose birthing had caused his beloved wife's death? Opposing waves of anguish and love must have rolled over him. But he did not deny God because there was no justice in a woman's death in childbirth. He did not try to make things right by his own actions; he knew that he could not.

To know that we need to be transfused with the blood of the Lamb is not to succumb to illness, but to move toward health. Along with the revivifying transfusion is given an understanding that we are all part of the butterfly effect. As long as there is any pain in the universe, the Creator is part of that pain, and we bear our own small part in carrying it. It is bearable as long as the burden is shared.

And if in the fullness of God's time, Lucifer and Michael are again friends, there will be no more echthroi.

No echthroi. I think of those two men in criminal court, and pray for their healing. For my own letting go of residual anger and hurt, and my acceptance that I have often been betrayer rather than betrayed. Perfection of virtue is not required of me. Perfection of love is, and that is a very different thing. Jesus said, "What I want is mercy, not sacrifice." How wonderful! Christ did not come into the world to save the virtuous, but to save you, and me, and Jacob (lying with his head pillowed on a stone), and Ikhnaton, with his psalms of praise for the One God, and all of us who turn to the Source of all love, knowing that we need to be transfused.

Jacob was weak and he knew that he was weak; nevertheless he would not leave off wrestling until the angel blessed him

239

with the wound of love.

God's angel wrestles with us, and we cry out, "Bless me!" And God will bless us and we, like the baboons, will clap our hands and cry out our joy as we join in the glorious music of the spheres. In this harmony we will no longer be separated from the stars, and we will be at-one, too, with the infinitely small things of creation. In this communion we will be blessed indeed.

A jury room in Manhattan's criminal court, January, 1984
Wheaton, Illinois, October, 1985

17 disaster —
18 — Hour of God Sep Sm
— Cross — stars
— melanie
41 — moving on
— beyond tribalism — not safe
42
42\ interrelatedness of
universe "butterfly effect"
→ malignant independence
(cancerous cells)
33 — Trying to be good
58 — Listen — begin courage
to do God's will — small along RA
51 — Prayer — away fm forensic/RA
approach — Listen